Literary Power and the Criteria of Truth

Literary Power and the Criteria of Truth

Laura Quinney

Foreword by Harold Bloom

University Press of Florida

Gainesville / Tallahassee / Tampa / Boca Raton
Pensacola / Orlando / Miami / Jacksonville

Copyright 1995 by the Board of Regents of the State of Florida
Printed in the United States of America on acid-free paper ∞
All rights reserved

00 99 98 97 96 95   6 5 4 3 2 1

Library of Congress Cataloging-in-Publication Data
Quinney, Laura.
Literary power and the criteria of truth/by Laura Quinney;
foreword by Harold Bloom.
p.   cm.
Includes bibliographical references and index.
ISBN 0-8130-1345-3
1. English literature—History and criticism—Theory, etc.
2. Literature—History and criticism—Theory, etc.   3. Literature—
Philosophy.   4. Truth in literature.   5. Canon (Literature)
6. Tragic, The.   I. Title.
PR21.Q56   1995
820.9—dc20   94-42895

The University Press of Florida is the scholarly publishing agency
for the State University System of Florida, comprised of Florida A & M University,
Florida Atlantic University, Florida International University, Florida State University,
University of Central Florida, University of Florida, University of North Florida,
University of South Florida, and University of West Florida.

University Press of Florida
15 Northwest 15th Street
Gainesville, FL 32611

For Billy

Contents

Foreword, by Harold Bloom / ix

Preface / xiii

INTRODUCTION
Wittgenstein and the Prestige of Tragic Sense / 1

CHAPTER 1
Weil and Aeschylus / 13

CHAPTER 2
Johnson in Mourning / 29

CHAPTER 3
The Grimness of the Truth /

CHAPTER 4
Daimonic Splendor / 87

CHAPTER 5
Shelley's Fate / 123

CHAPTER 6
Wittgenstein's Melancholy / 145

Notes / 169

Works Cited / 175

Index / 181

Foreword

> After the fire was well kindled . . . more wine was poured over Shelley's dead body than he had consumed during his life. This with the oil and salt made the yellow flames glisten and quiver. The heat from the sun and fire was so intense that the atmosphere was tremulous and wavy. The corpse fell open and the heart was laid bare.
>
> —*Trelawney*

Shelley's funeral pyre is one of those points of sublimity where life and literature seem to exchange perspectives. Trelawney and Byron gave their friend the final tribute of an appropriate ceremony, wordless yet profoundly Shelleyan. The aura of that beach scene lingers in our consciousness of Shelley's achievement, which goes beyond even the poet's actual originality, strong as that was both cognitively and imagistically. The *idea* of Shelley perhaps transcends his own visions: something remorseless, uncompromising, defiant, abides with us. That is not quite our idea of Dr. Johnson, a wisdom writer more akin to Koheleth than to a High Romantic prophet. Nor do either Shelley or Johnson much resemble Simone Weil, a Jewish spiritual who found nothing to sustain her in the Hebrew Bible, and who somehow assimilated Jesus to Homer and to Aeschylus. Little as Shelley, Johnson, and Weil share, in temperament or in thought, the philosopher Ludwig Wittgenstein at first seems farthest removed from all of them, emerging as he does from Schopenhauer. Laura Quinney disarmingly begins by observing that her choice of authors in this book is an "unlikely" one. A tragic sense of life, "the grimness of the truth," is her context for studying these figures together. And yet there is an acuteness of religious concern that binds Quinney's writers, though she declines to see that as her subject, or rather she centers, subtly and intensely, just outside of the religious sphere, in a Blanchotian sense of the vocation of the writer. If Weil had that vocation, I must be blind to it. As Quinney indicates, Weil thought that only the Fool spoke truth in *King Lear;* I am puzzled why Weil did not locate the tragedy's true outcast in Edgar, recalcitrant and enduring until the end, and surely the prophet of the play's ultimate wisdom:

> Men must endure
> Their going hence even as their coming hither,
> Ripeness is all.

The grimness of the truth nowhere else is expressed with such authority, but Weil (as Quinney hints) had a fiercely narrow notion of truth. The appropriateness of Weil for Quinney's argument is not in question, but I wonder how well the self-outcast waiter-for-God sustains close juxtaposition with a great lyric poet, a superb moral critic, and a central philosopher of language. It is the *choice* of Weil by Quinney that surprises me, and I want to explore the choice here as a path into Quinney's poignant and eloquent study of the Sublime. Why take Weil rather than say Kafka, upon whom Quinney has written elsewhere with impressively individual insight?

Dr. Johnson, who sensibly dreaded dying, hardly would have approved Weil's formulation which Quinney quotes to conclude her chapter on that secular saint: "To love the truth means to endure the void, and, as a result, to accept death. Truth is on the side of death." That reductiveness is reconcilable with Freud's "reality-testing" and perhaps with Shelley's Lucretianism, but is hardly Christian. Yet it is Schopenhauerian enough to be acceptable to Wittgenstein, and on an uncanny level doubtless approximates an ultimate Johnsonian anxiety. If Johnson shares Koheleth's wisdom, it is partly at the expense of participating also in the implicit nihilism of Ecclesiastes. That may be why Quinney is driven to include Weil, scarcely of the eminence of Johnson, Shelley, and Wittgenstein, but a powerful instance of a worship of the void deluding itself into an outcast version of New Testament spirituality. If you seek a representation of the grimness of the truth, then Weil's negative clarity has undoubted appeal.

Wittgenstein's distrust of the tragic paradigm, as emphasized by Quinney, is vindicated by Simone Weil's spurious authority. Though Quinney will not say so, Weil is one of Wittgenstein's "captivating pictures," a misrepresentation of reality. Melancholy—whether in Johnson, Shelley, or Wittgenstein (or in Freud)—is a very different mode of temperament than is Weil's outcast self-election. Quinney finally is more Wittgensteinian than de Manian in her critical orientation, and even more Shelleyan and Johnsonian in her own linguistic skepticism. Her criticism has absorbed the lesson taught by Wittgenstein's own bafflement by Shakespeare. Freud obsessed Wittgenstein, who nevertheless was able to partly dismiss the Freudian mode of interpretation as "a powerful mythology." Shakespeare was not to be dismissed, and in some desperation Wittgenstein decided that Shakespeare was not so much a poet as "creator of language." But what is that? It is only a trope for a creator of culture and value, and so for a creator of meaning. Quinney's book is at once a highly individual reflection of advanced critical praxis, and even more vitally a return to what uniquely makes literary criticism literary rather than a social science or a philosophy. *Literary Power and the Criteria of Truth* follows Shelley in recognizing that demystifiction can be a process destructive of literary value, and also follows Johnson in realizing that literary affect can be the highest form of mourning. Laura Quinney's first book goes a long way toward achieving a vitalizing stance in relation to the wisdom of literary tradition.

Harold Bloom

Preface

—O'er many a dark and dreary vale
 They pass'd, and many a region dolorous;
O'er many a frozen, many a fiery Alp;
Rocks, caves, lakes, fens, bogs, dens and shades of death,
 A universe of death.

The subject of this book was in a sense first broached by later-eighteenth-century reflections on tragedy and sublimity. For it was then that the emerging disciplines of literary criticism and aesthetics began to be fascinated by the literary power and philosophical authority of the tragic sense. The sad or tragic or darkly sublime was characterized as the telos of literature. Almost all the literary quotations in Burke's *Enquiry* concern the grim and disturbing subject matter of the sublime: terror, exile, intimidation, diminishment, and loss. Burke also had the beautiful to consider, and he does include a few quotations to exemplify its nature. But, just as his account of the beautiful is shorter and less engaged than his treatment of the sublime, so his literary elucidations of beauty are fewer and less impressive. This asymmetry follows a logical consequence of his argument, since he has identified sublimity with power and hence implicitly with whatever might make a literary moment striking and memorable. How could evocations of the beautiful have any literary force? Though Burke does not quite openly acknowledge it, he has ranged the mode of effect proper to literature on the side of the sublime.

This secret conflation of literary excellence with the drama and discomfort of sublimity emerges in the last section of his treatise, called "Of Words." There Burke sets out to analyze literary language and, in his terms, its peculiar "powers." He addresses himself particularly to the question of "how words influence the passions" and why they are "able to affect us as strongly as the things they represent, and sometimes much more strongly." As examples of such strong "influence," he chooses only passages on sublime topics, including the passage from *Paradise Lost* quoted above. The subject matter of sublimity is obscurity, danger, and death, threatening phenomena that, as Burke says, activate the self-preservative instincts. Perhaps he is right that fearful subject matter moves us most because it concerns what is ultimately most important to us. But in the case of literary language, it is not only disturbing subject matter that may produce the sublime but something also in the form or nature of the language itself and thus something uncanny in its very capacity to affect. From this capacity it acquires a magistry and mystery only dimly related to the phenomenal manifestations of power and obscurity that Burke had anatomized earlier.

Burke is impressed by the passage from *Paradise Lost* because Milton boldly subsumes the elements of the natural landscape—rocks, caves, lakes, and so on—to "death": "This idea or this affection caused by a word, which nothing but a word could annex to the others, raises a very great degree of the sublime; and this sublime is raised yet higher by what follows, a *'universe of death.'* Here are again two ideas not presentable but by language; and an union of them great and amazing beyond conception." Burke describes as sublime both the gloomy subject matter and the mode of literary representation. His argument may seem somewhat confused, but I think he has recognized something significant without quite articulating it: he perceives that there is some natural or inherent match between the forbidding subject matter most likely to affect us and the nature and mode of the effect that literary language already aspires to. Rather than reflecting grimness, literature has to seek out grim subject matter—the universe of death—to make itself commanding to us. And in order to summon up a somber resonance, it need not depend on mimetically reproducing what is somber in the world; it may instead elaborate "ideas not presentable but by language." Literature is in the business of affecting *by way of* disturbance and trouble: in no other way, even where these affects are only "caused by a word, which nothing but a word" could cause.

And yet, as Gilles Deleuze has said, "an indescribable joy always rushes out of great books, even when they speak of ugly, hopeless, or terrifying things" (19). Whether it is to be called an experience of pathos or sublimity or tragic sense, there is a satisfaction in being grieved by literature, as Burke's enthusiasm for the "universe of death" implies. This surprising combination of affects was precisely the feature of the sublime that intrigued eighteenth-century aestheticians. It provided the philosophically interesting contradiction, the puzzle, that attracted figures like Burke and, later, Kant. The "natural" sublime was assimilated to the older "literary" sublime because of what was perceived to be their common ambivalence. As a special case of literary affect, the paradoxical pleasure of tragedy—as identified by Burke, Hume, and Kames, among others—gave the clearest example of such an ambivalence.

This book relates the attractions of the tragic sense and its general ascendancy to the influence of its literary derivation. In contrast to later eighteenth-century aesthetic theory, I am applying the broadest meaning to the words "tragic" and "tragic sense" here: my use of these terms has nothing to do with generic definition, and it probably ranges beyond what the genre of tragedy would suggest. For I will treat "tragic sense" as interchangeable with the conviction of the grimness of the truth. The arguments of this book are based on the premise that the literature most likely to be seen as "deep" or "real" or "true" is tragic literature—not only tragedies per se but works of all genres that seem bent on impressing us with the dark view. According to this hierarchy of literary value, *King Lear* ranks above *The Tempest, Clarissa* above *Pamela,* and Shelley's *The Triumph of Life* above *Prometheus Unbound.* (These rankings are easy and orthodox, yet the tragic kind of literature can also include works that are technically comic, so long as they represent their comic sensibility as a stay against crueler certainties.) The works at the top of the hierarchy have the prestige of serious, philosophical thought. They earn this prestige precisely because they adopt a bleak perspective and deny our hopes. A more optimistic view, indeed any view that resists this one, is represented as willful illusion. These works derive conviction from confirming our fears; to use a contemporary dialect, they are demystifying. Their pessimism, gravity, and glamour go hand in hand. For underlying this hierarchy of value is a concept of truth's province, an assumption that it will turn out to be just what we would not wish, something sad and disheartening. Literature that corroborates this sense of truth is held in the highest esteem.

These remarks should strike the reader as commonplace. If these *are* basic assumptions about the destiny of literature and the character of the truth, they should seem so obvious as not to need uttering. But just because they seem natural does not mean that they are; as Wittgenstein sometimes does in *Philosophical Investigations,* I will ask you to "let yourself be struck" by the assumptions exposed here. Isn't it strange that the tragic sense should be privileged, and associated with literary value?

There are many works on the theory of tragedy and many more that confirm the accuracy or prevalence of the tragic sense; but it has not been usual to investigate the relation between the authority of the tragic sense and its literary provenance—or to question it, at any rate. I will use the name "the tragic paradigm" to designate this complex of associations: the idea that the truth must take a tragic form and its corroboration or institution by means of literary pathos. I take the term "paradigm" from Wittgenstein, who uses it to signify the range of meanings a word takes within a language-game and the ideas, assumptions, and ways of living that flow from this complex of meanings.

Wittgenstein provides a philosophical precedent for the kind of argument I make here; I will be exploring the relevance of his later philosophy in my introduction. The literary-critical sources of this argument may be less apparent. Its most immediate relative would perhaps be the study of the literary sublime, especially in those critics who assume that there is, as Burke thought, a mode of power or an affect proper to literary language. Those who do would include Longinus, of course, as well as Bloom, Hertz, and Lacoue-Labarthe, though probably not Weiskel, Ferguson, or Zizek. Some studies of the sublime are allied to de Manian deconstruction for the good reason that it too treats literary language as unique and effectual, indeed capable of promoting grave metaphysical errors and blindness, including the concealment and mystification of its own nature.

I claim that under the tragic paradigm the criteria of literary power inculcate a notion of truth that is then mistakenly taken to be mimetic. Although my terms are more general, this claim bears a family resemblance to the notions of linguistic mystification and deception in de Manian deconstruction. But there are some significant differences. I do not attribute the confusion of truth and tragic affect to any inevitable linguistic predicament. Nor is it my intention to produce any theses about the ontological status of language. Conversely, de Manian deconstruction would object to my emphasis on literary affect and to other frankly psychological aspects of this inquiry, since it would consider any such terms to be strictly tropological. But I would argue in response that the epistemological skepticism entertained by de Manian deconstruction derives its own satisfactions from participating in the tragic paradigm. The famous severity, wrongly called nihilism, and the authority of asceticism and deprivation in de Man's essays fulfill the requirement for discomfort under which a certain kind of "truth" can be recognized. Of course, adherence to the tragic paradigm is not unique to de Man among analytical writers. It is often quite openly embraced by critics with a belletristic bent—by those, that is, who aspire to literary quality in their own work, if only in imitation of or fidelity to the literature they discuss. The appearance of the tragic paradigm is more remarkable in de Man because it is enhanced by means of his self-representation as a philosophical (and not a literary) writer.

The general influence of de Manian deconstruction on this work is in part explained by the presence of a shared influence, that of the French philosopher and critic Maurice Blanchot. It was Blanchot who described "l'espace littéraire" as a strange and solitary space in which authors encounter the demands of their own vocation and are pressed by its autonomous and sovereign "exigency." Blanchot himself has perhaps developed these ideas out of their adumbrations in Kafka and Proust. He has attempted to be faithful to the nature of "literary space" as he has evoked it and so has written a direct but lyrical style that is, in a positive sense, essayistic. My own style has been inspired in its aspirations by Blanchot's.

It accords with the argument of this book that so broad a range of authors as Burke, de Man, Wittgenstein, and Blanchot should respond to the same literary fascination. In the course of my discussion, I will be exploring the sources of the tragic sense and its peculiar authority, especially the authority it exerts over literature and through literature. This problematic, somewhat baffling or barren in the abstract, takes its interest from the role it plays in the work of specific authors. I will be studying a number of authors, indeed a wide and unlikely combination of them—Percy Shelley, Ludwig Wittgenstein, Samuel Johnson, and Simone Weil. It is strange, of course, to move from Weil to Johnson and stranger still to move from Johnson to Shelley. In historical context, intellectual interests, politics, vocabulary, and genres of writing, these figures could hardly seem more remote. But their differences are not everything. An important affinity lies in a feature of their writing (and writing is all they are now): there remains the particular ambition reflected in the characteristic affect of their work, in their themes, and in their style. Weil, Johnson, and Shelley each strive, after his or her own fashion, to arrive at an effective, individual restatement of the grimness of the truth. They were all devoted readers; and they all aim to appropriate for their own style, or re-create in their own style, the shock of disappointment and pain that their reading had shown them to be the affect constitutive of literary power.

The discussion is framed by studies of Wittgenstein and Weil, philosophers whose interest in tragic thought both illuminates and betrays the literary advantage of equating sorrow and truth. Longer studies focus on Johnson and Shelley, authors who were deeply engaged with the promises of literature (and therefore sometimes mistrustful of them). Literary ardor takes a similar form in each, and their sense of what the truth will look like, when it is found, remains the same. For Johnson and for Shelley, to have wrestled the difficulties of truth to expression is to have uncovered something that we do not want to hear and at the same time, strangely, to have fulfilled the requirements of literary expertise. That even these two could share this paradigm testifies to its general force, invisible otherwise in so far as it is axiomatic.

The choice of these two authors is significant because of the extent to which they represent the influences behind contemporary habits of critical thought and literary taste. Johnson was an inventor of modern criticism; Shelley was a legislator and fierce exponent of Romantic taste. They come from periods that are regarded as distinct and from literary cultures regarded as antithetical, yet they agreed implicitly on the task of literature. In this way, their relation defies the artificial severing of Romanticism from its later-eighteenth-century context. Whatever historical moment evolved the grimness of the truth, it is not, as one might expect, strictly a Romantic or post-Romantic phenomenon. Twentieth-century preoccupations and tastes may have made the phenomenon palpable, yet it predates not just us but the Romantics who would seem to have formed our literary assumptions.

The juxtaposition of such various figures reflects a considered strategy of synthesis, for my argument is precisely that these authors from diverse periods and diverse contexts read the same works and responded to the same literary imperative: to reproduce "the grimness of the truth" as it had been embodied in the literature they prized. We would expect the sense of what counts as "tragic" to be affected by the historical traumas of the twentieth century, yet Weil herself claimed a continuity of her feeling for the tragic with that expressed in authors as historically remote, and as different from each other and from her as Homer, St. John of the Cross, and Shakespeare. The striking fact is that the historical difference did not affect the authors' common definition of the desiderata of writing. One purpose of this book is to explore how this universalizing sense of the task of literature, and its proper grimness, emerges out of literary experience. It is all the more remarkable that Johnson, Weil, and Shelley should share assumptions about the nature of literary power when they occupied such disparate historical milieu.

Johnson, Weil, and Shelley are clearly not the only writers who show a desire to re-create the grimness of the truth. It is a common aspiration, though more pressing or univocal in some authors than others. It seems particularly vivid in Wyatt, Hardy, Chekhov, and Beckett, to name a few. But it is not yet clear what variables of historical period, genre, and temperament determine the strength of this aspiration. Accordingly, the choice of authors here is meant to be representative rather than inclusive. Yet in arguing that these authors were moved by the same imperative, I do not mean to suggest that they responded to it identically. Indeed, my discussion follows the path of increasing self-consciousness and skepticism about the grimness of the truth, and increasingly deliberate, if futile efforts to resist it; Weil was the most willing adherent of the tragic paradigm, while Johnson was more suspicious of it, Shelley questioned it, and Wittgenstein critiqued it outright. But even in the case of the latter two the paradigm maintained its hold, because their very rebellion against the grimness of the truth reflected the intensity of their secret belief in it. My design here is not so much to make a linear argument as to study the distinctive manifestations of the phenomenon in each author, in such a way that the studies touch and separate, vary, overlap, and retrace dark forms whose shape and presence grows with acquaintance more intuitable.

I would like to thank Mary Jacobus, Cynthia Chase, and Jonathan Culler for their comments on the first version of this manuscript. I am grateful to Laura Brown, who was the director of my dissertation; nor could I have wished for a more helpful adviser. Harold Bloom showed me how I might take literary affect seriously, as did Neil Hertz, with whom I first studied Johnson. Steven Shaviro urged me to read both Wittgenstein and Blanchot (among others, such as Proust, who make a quieter appearance in this book). I have had many wonderful conversations about Johnson with Thomas Reinert. Burton Dreben and Stanley Cavell educated me in different versions of Wittgenstein. I also learned much about Wittgenstein from the members of an informal reading group, which included Juliet Floyd, Eli Friedlander, Steven Gerrard, and Moshe Halbertal. But any errors with regard to Wittgenstein, and any misprisons, are my own. I wish to thank Walter Cohen, Deborah Gordon, Leslie Kurke, Jeff Nunokawa, Richard Moran, Paul Morrison, and Joseph Weiss for their kind advice and encouragement.

I am grateful to Cornell University for a Sage Graduate Fellowship and to the Society of Fellows at Harvard for several years of intellectual stimulation and financial support.

My greatest debt, in thought and morale, is to my husband, William Flesch.

INTRODUCTION

Wittgenstein and the Prestige of Tragic Sense

> Where was it one first heard of the truth? The the.
>
> *Wallace Stevens*, "The Man on the Dump"

In his later philosophy, Wittgenstein develops the technique of reducing our assumptions to self-evident generalizations—"tautologies," he calls them, and also grammatical or "concept-forming" propositions—whose "obviousness" is revealed thereby and simultaneously unmasked. These are the assumptions that seem natural and inevitable because they govern our concepts and provide the grounds of judgment. I am following the mode of thought and some of the strategies of Wittgenstein's later philosophy in suggesting that there is an (arbitrary) concept of truth intertwined with our concept of literature. Actually, Wittgenstein himself came to suspect the authority of the tragic paradigm in the course of reflecting on other analytical writers and their fundamental assumptions. I am indebted to his writings in many different ways, but most clearly, perhaps most deeply, I am indebted to this scrutiny of the tragic paradigm and its force.

In 1931 Wittgenstein wrote a series of "remarks" on Frazer's *Golden Bough*. He devoted particular attention to an ancient practice that Frazer opens his book by describing: at Nemi, a King of the Wood was appointed to stand guard over a sacred tree; yet his guardianship consisted only of thwarting attacks by his competitors, one of whom would eventually prevail against him, kill him, and succeed to his office. Wittgenstein offers a number of observations about this legendary ritual:

And here the explanation is not what satisfies us anyway. When Frazer begins by telling the story of the King of the Wood at Nemi, he does this in a tone which shows that something strange and terrible is happening here. And that is the answer to the question "why is this happening?": Because it is terrible. In other words, what strikes us in this course of events as terrible, impressive, horrible, tragic, &c., anything but trivial and insignificant, *that* is what gave birth to them.

We can only *describe* and say, human life is like that.

Put that account of the King of the Wood at Nemi together with the phrase "the majesty of death," and you see they are one.
    The life of the priest-king shows what is meant by that phrase.

If someone is gripped by the majesty of death, then through such a life he can give expression to it.—Of course this is not an explanation: it puts one symbol in place of another. Or one ceremony in place of another. (*Remarks on Frazer's Golden Bough* 2–3)

Wittgenstein does not make the familiar observation that the ritual can be described by the phrase "the majesty of death" but chooses instead to make the opposite claim, an unusual and somewhat obscure one, that "the life of the priest-king shows what is meant by that phrase." We know what it means to say that a phrase exemplifies the nature of an event, ritual, or way of life but not what it means to say the reverse, that the life exemplifies a phrase. Wittgenstein goes on to refine this strange logic by asserting that the life and the phrase are "symbols" or "ceremonies" of the same order, a claim implying that "life" is not simply a natural fact, nor language simply its symbolic expression. The phrase "majesty of death" is being accorded some generative power of its own, some power of the phrase over and above its semantic content.

In one of his own powerfully opaque phrases, Wittgenstein asserted that "to imagine a language means to imagine a form of life." And the major work of his later philosophy, *Philosophical Investigations*, explores the delicate question of language's role in creating and sustaining "the forms of life." Wittgenstein's analysis of the King of the Wood and his fate seems to offer an early, shadowy reconnaissance of this issue, in which the language of "majesty" and "death" predicates a "strange and terrible," "impressive, horrible, tragic" life.

This early appearance of an issue critical to the *Investigations* is intriguing because of the subject's grave drama and the grave poetry of the phrase "majesty of death." The phrase must be majestic itself in order for it to compel this uncanny "expression" in ritual; its majesty is that of literature's severe style, the style intertwined with the tragic paradigm. Here Wittgenstein suggests that through its ritual the culture shows itself to be in the grip of this paradigm, acting out its fascination with a dark and powerful phrase.

It is hard to tell whether, at the time that he wrote these remarks, Wittgenstein still respected this authority of the "terrible" and "tragic"—for his comments seem to stand in awe of their subject, despite their analytical character—but they do clear the path for his later suspicions of the tragic sense. These suspicions, which deeply influenced the style and structure of *Philosophical Investigations* as well as its argument, he expressed most succinctly in his response to psychoanalysis.

Wittgenstein's remarks about psychoanalysis exemplify his sense of how an analytical argument, with its own picture of the truth, might hold us captive. In conversations with Rush Rhees during the 1940s, he criticized Freud's mythmaking, his reliance on the paradigm of determinism, and his representation of psychoanalysis as empirical science. He reproved Freud's confusion of speculation with science, not out of any reverence for science—far from it—but out of a suspicion of ideas that derive their "attractiveness" from sources that they do not acknowledge. Psychoanalysis, he suggested, tells a compelling story whose power of persuasion flows from its recourse to determinism. Wittgenstein was highly skeptical of psychological determinism, of the notion that the psyche, too, must have its laws; this is not surprising since, in rethinking his earlier work as a mathematical logician, he had also become suspicious of the too-easily applied "laws of logic" and of the notion that rules govern the use of language. "Whereas to me," he said in answer to psychoanalysis, "the fact that there *aren't* actually any laws seems important" (*Lectures* 42). He suggested that bold, systemic, "deep" generalization wins conviction on its own, especially when it reverts to "mythological" patterns of circularity, identity, and repetition. Determinism brings relief to the mind, and so one tends to accede with strange comfort to deterministic generalizations.

> Freud in his analysis provides explanations which many people are inclined to accept. He emphasizes that people are *dis*-inclined to accept them. But if the explanation is one which people are disinclined to accept, it is highly probable that it is also one which they are *inclined* to accept. And this is what Freud had actually brought out. Take Freud's view that anxiety is always a repetition in some way of the anxiety we felt at birth. He does not establish this by reference to evidence—for he could not do so. But it is an idea which has a marked attraction. It has the attraction that mythological explanations have, explanations which say that this is all a repetition of something that has happened before. And when people do accept or adopt this, then certain things seem much clearer and easier for them. (*Lectures* 43)

Through their appeal to determinism, Freud's radically counterintuitive claims paradoxically assert the power of intuitions. The dark insights of psychoanalysis beguile us with their appeal to rich, tragic patterning: "Much the same could be said of the notion of an 'Urszene.' This often has the attractiveness of giving a sort of tragic pattern to one's life. It is all the repetition of the same pattern which was settled long ago. Like a tragic figure carrying out the decrees under which the fates had placed him at birth." (*Lectures* 51). This picture is so attractive as to be mesmerizing, authoritative, and therefore dangerous: "Analysis is likely to do harm. Because although one may discover in the course of it various things about oneself, one must have a very strong and keen and persistent criticism in order to recognize and see through the mythology that is offered or imposed on one. There is an inducement to say, 'Yes, of course, it must be like that.' A powerful mythology" (*Lectures* 51–52).

These musingly critical remarks must be read in light of Wittgenstein's describing himself as "a disciple of Freud" and "a follower of Freud"

(*Lectures* 41). According to Rhees, "Freud was one of the few authors he thought worth reading" (*Lectures* 41). We should interpret his critique of psychoanalysis not as a polemical attack on it, but as a self-searching reflection on a theory whose intellectual force he acknowledged to be considerable. Here, as in most of his writing, Wittgenstein can be seen combating the "mythologies" that he found enticing to his own mind, for his thought developed out of his resistance to them. Thus, in reflecting on Freud's power, Wittgenstein uses the same paradigms of temptation and "imposition" that he uses to describe the workings of language. Language is itself a purveyor of "powerful mythologies," as Wittgenstein suggested in his famous aphorism "Philosophy is a battle against the bewitchment of our intelligence by means of language" (no. 109).[1]

According to Wittgenstein, the power of psychoanalysis lies in its having the force of mythology at the same time that it professes to be empirical science. It achieves its power by effacing its fictional (or "mythological") status; that is, it lays claim to truth-value by playing the language-game of propositional truth (without acknowledging that it is a game). Though propositions are in general said to act in this way, the example of psychoanalysis stands out because it leads Wittgenstein to wonder about the attractiveness and the truthfulness of specifically tragic or deterministic paradigms. In general, Wittgenstein attempted to investigate the origin of our assumptions about the nature of the truth—our assumptions, that is, about what form it is likely to take, where it can be found, and how it will feel to discover it. My own work is very much inspired by this skeptical inquiry into our definition of the truth.

Suspicious of the naive confidence and dogmatism he accused himself of displaying in his early work, Wittgenstein came to see that a powerful sense of truth—a kind of "affect of truth" (not that he would have ever used such a phrase)—might exert itself through spurious means. Wittgenstein probed the question of the status of the truth, asking to what extent our sense of the truth's shape and provenance is guided by arbitrary features of language-games. First of all, he questioned the intellectual forms under which we recognize truth claims as legitimate. In rejecting the approach of the *Tractatus*, Wittgenstein had come to doubt the trustworthiness of explanatory rigor and the superior truth-value of logic. "In what sense is logic something sublime?" (no. 89), he asks, meaning, how is it that logic comes to strike us as shimmering, transcendental, and eternally true? For Wittgenstein, "sublimity" spells mystification, the error into which we fall through the misguided search for metaphysical, or "higher," truth. He goes on to expose the "rigor" of logic as a chimera produced by a preconceived attachment to "crystalline purity" (no. 108), that purity that betokens the transcendental and the sublime. Yet logic cannot exert a privileged claim to truth when "giving grounds [or] justifying the evidence, comes to an end;—but the end is not certain propositions' striking us immediately as true, i.e., it is not a kind of *seeing* on our part; it is our *acting*, which lies at the bottom of the language-game" (*On Certainty* no. 204). Though we offer "logic" as grounds for our convictions, it is not logic that originally determined them or that actually sustains them—it is not seeing, or intellectual perception, but deep-rooted habit and training that convince us to go on in the same way. But it is precisely because of its "crystalline purity" that logic persuades us of its truth, just as, according to the musings above, tragic determinism provides the attraction of psychoanalysis.

Generalizations and global arguments require us by their very form to consider their truth-value. They derive force from the assumption that language attempts to correspond to extralinguistic "truth"—and this is precisely the assumption that Wittgenstein calls into question, at the same time that both the form and the method of *Philosophical Investigations* enact his mistrust of generalization. Some paragraphs in the *Investigations* scrutinize the intertwining of propositions with truth claims. Wittgenstein rejects the *Tractatus* picture of language's irreducible nugget, "the general form of propositions," and suggests instead that it is our concept of the proposition, a concept no more fixed and bounded than our concept of language or game, that happens to include the predication of truth or falsity. As for the so-called "general form of propositions"—that is, the sentence—"This is how things are," Wittgenstein roundly asserts: "To say that this proposition agrees (or does not agree) with reality would be obvious nonsense," but it shows that "*one* feature of our concept of a proposition is, *sounding like a proposition*" (no. 134). Whatever lays claim to the form of a proposition purports to assert a truth-value, but this claim is based on its form, which also means what we take that form to signify. The proposition is that which has the form of an assertion and with which we play the language-game of mimesis: "What a proposition is is in one sense determined by the rules of sentence formation (in English, for example), and in another sense by the use of the sign in the language-game" (no. 136). The rules of sentence formation establish, more or less, what will count as a proposition (until these rules are intentionally or accidentally revised), but what the proposition will count as is established by the use we make of it (until the language-game mutates or we change our minds). The language-game of generalization exerts its own appeal, to whose aid propositions come, bringing their elegant form.

The power of the tragic paradigm is clearly intertwined with the power of generalization, since it is in generalizations that the tragic sense expresses itself (whether or not they are explicitly articulated). Wittgenstein criticized the "craving for generality" that, springing from a mistaken reverence for scientific method, had in his opinion instilled many philosophers and other serious thinkers such as Freud with wrongheaded and damaging aspirations.[2] It was a major part of his own method to show the poverty of generalization and to eschew the reductions of systemization. In fact, he thought at one time of using Kent's line in *King Lear* "I'll teach you differences" as an epigraph to the *Investigations*. Wittgenstein was therefore intent on analyzing and exposing the mystique of generalizing propositions. His remarks on psychoanalysis may also suggest that he saw the relation between the attractions of generalization and the attractions of the tragic paradigm. In any case, that they are related—and related specifically through the prestige of the generalizing overview—is an assumption of this book, which analyses the appeal of tragic generalization and the nourishment it derives from literature.

In describing a certain kind of mathematical question, posed when the mode of its solution is unknown, Wittgenstein argued that this kind of question is like a riddle,

> like the problem set by the king in the fairy tale who told the princess to come neither naked nor dressed and she came wearing fishnet. That might have been called not naked and not dressed either. He didn't really know what he wanted her to do, but when she came

thus he was forced to accept it. It was of the form "Do something which I shall be inclined to call 'neither naked nor dressed.'" It's the same with the mathematical problem. "Do something which I shall be inclined to accept as a solution, though I don't know now what it will be like."[3]

Borrowing the logic of Wittgenstein's analysis, I suggest that we have a relation of this kind to the truth as it is elaborated under the tragic paradigm; we are looking in advance for representations that will strike us as true, and they will strike us in this way if they meet implicit, amorphous, and to some extent arbitrary preestablished criteria. The criteria for what will count as the truth under the tragic paradigm are derived from literature, where they are formed by the conditions peculiar to that medium—that is, by the pathos or severity or "sublimity" that gives it force. (Obviously there is a potential confusion of terms here: "pathos" is not identical with "severity" and is perhaps not the best name for the affect of grimness and sternness, or sometimes sadness and rue, that I am arguing certain works strive for. But "pathos" is practically the only relevant word in our limited terminology of literary affect. As to knowing what affect is at issue, the word "sublime" unfortunately begs the question.)

Wittgenstein's suspicion of the allurement in generalizations that, like Freud's, set out to be commanding and disturbing and that compel our assent for this reason, may have helped lead him to the important critique of metaphysical skepticism in *On Certainty*. There he explores the attractions of the skeptical perspective, as he had done with the tragic paradigm. He represents skepticism as a form of idea that falls in with criteria of truth established by conventions of our language.[4] This critique of skepticism has immediate relevance to our critique of the tragic paradigm, for Johnson and Shelley's shared belief in the grimness of the truth is reflected by the skeptical elements in their work. What these skeptical elements conceal is a deeper conviction, however resisted, that the truth will take the bitter, disenchanting form that skepticism promises. And this conviction is related, in turn, to the authority of the philosophical overview, the force of generalizations, and the charm of pathos, a specifically literary quality that exerts its attraction over all writers.

Wittgenstein shows the way to undercutting the paradigm of tragic necessity. The grimness of the truth is—to use Wittgenstein's dramatic language—a "powerful mythology," a mesmerizing picture drawn by our language-games and holding us captive. But, though Wittgenstein may have wished to discredit and dispel the magic of the tragic paradigm, he could not do so for himself. Like Shelley, he remains haunted by a sense of skeptical disappointment in spite of his effort to question the intellectual power of skepticism. And again like Shelley's, Wittgenstein's suspicion of the tragic paradigm seems proportionally related to the intensity of the attraction the tragic sense held for him. He was a despairing figure, as is well known. In contradistinction to the dominant trend of Wittgenstein interpretation, I propose that Wittgenstein's literary power, like Freud's, is of a tragic cast and that even his resistance to overarching generalization found itself unable to escape the enchantments of tragic affect.

The first question one wants to ask about the appearance of the tragic paradigm in literary texts—particularly in works of such intellectual authority as Johnson's and Shelley's—is, isn't it true? Isn't life really as bad as they say? Why should one isolate their pessimism and attribute it to the shaping of a paradigm? The representational or mimetic dimension of literature encourages us to see the sad view as descriptive of reality—colored perhaps by individual temperament or vision, but essentially accurate. Yet even if pessimism strikes us as realistic, the pursuit of mimesis does not explain the degree of intensity, insistence, elaboration, and effort of refinement in works that adhere to the tragic paradigm. However true what they seem to say is, they didn't have to say it, and certainly not so precisely and deeply and obsessively: their labor to refine and improve on the tragic sense betokens obedience to some imperative other than accuracy. And again we must wonder why their gloominess should seem so natural and inevitable.

Wittgenstein's thinking might help us here to reconceive the compelling appearances of mimesis. His later philosophy wrestles with a related problem, namely how to break the hold of the notion that language stands in a mirroring relationship to the world, that it "hooks on to the world," through an opaque, almost magical correspondence that eludes our frustrated understanding. This is the common picture of the way language works, but perhaps it is misguided; Wittgenstein suggests instead that language does not represent objects so much as objects provide "a means of representation" in language-games (*Philosophical Investigations* no. 50). Similarly, I would propose that material from experience provides a "means of grimness" for works committed to the tragic paradigm. We ought not to think of this paradigm as seeking to capture the reality of life—even if it does—but as capitalizing on its mimetic plausibility in order to consolidate its claims to literary power.[5]

Literature's mimetic appearances are of course prerequisite to its participation in the grimness of the truth. These appearances and our acceptance of them prove incorrigible; it is impossible to read without acceding to the mimetic dimension of language, at least provisionally. To go a step further: the (necessarily) representational orientation of literature encourages us to find some level at which we can take what it says to be true. We express our enchantment with literature in the belief that it tells the truth. Because this belief originates in an emotional commitment, so to speak, I call it "the love of mimesis." The force of the tragic paradigm begins in this commitment, which is constitutive, archaic, and intractable. The sense of truth is intertwined with the aspirations of literature (in so far as it constitutes representation; where else, after all, could we *see* the truth?). But the truth expressed by literature will be inflected by the enchantments of that medium. In this way tragic affect, with its independent aesthetic satisfactions, comes to influence our conception of the truth. Its influence is then ensured by a profoundly circular economy. The grimness of the truth draws on a remarkable, seemingly automatic authority; it derives its authority from the fact that it continues to be corroborated by what it is tested against: literature, its own source and home. Like Antaeus, the tragic paradigm returns to its ground to renew its strength.

This circular economy accounts for the tautological character of my observations about the interdependence of tragic sense and literary power. Many authors of high aspiration, authors who write in fidelity to their literary experience, will instinctively assume the task of recapturing and reproducing the grimness of the truth. The love of mimesis will put them on the path of believing, revolving, and reiterating the tragic paradigm. Weil, Johnson, and Shelley were authors of this kind: in their pursuit of sorrowful conclusions and innovative rhetorical style, each seeks to recreate the literary pathos by which they are transfixed. In the following chapters, I will be arguing that the tragic paradigm got its grip on these authors by way of their fascination with literature.

It takes some effort of thought to see the authority of tragic sense as factitious. This is the kind of effort Wittgenstein specialized in—getting under, or out from under, those of our assumptions that are like "bedrock."[6] For such an effort has its own prestige. Wittgenstein interrogated the high status of melancholy conclusions, and, en route to other philosophical problems, he seems to have reflected on the odd, instinctive power of the tragic, regarding that power as evidence of a presupposition—as paradigmatic rather than natural: we accede to tragic sense not so much because it captures the truth as because it forms a criterion for what we will be willing to count as the truth.

But here Wittgenstein's speculations reach a limit in their immediate usefulness to our project, for, naturally, it did not occur to him to attribute the authority of tragic sense to its literariness or to reflect on the ways in which the powers of literature and tragic sense might interact with and reinforce one another. He did not isolate the literary in a category of its own, and so he never considered that the tragic paradigm has a particularly literary provenance. He remained unconscious of the unique relation between literary power and the authority of tragic sense; and as a result of this innocence, a tragic note continues to resonate in his writing. The tragic paradigm proves its tenacity even in Wittgenstein's case, since his thought gravitates back to it in order to accommodate his aspirations after literary power.

His failure—or success, from another point of view—will be demonstrated in my last chapter. The intervening chapters on Johnson and Shelley explore that partnership of literature and the tragic paradigm that Wittgenstein did not recognize. First, however, I will examine a simpler test case—not in great detail, but briefly, I hope suggestively, as a means of sketching out some basic features of the phenomenon. My discussion of individual writers gets under way with this exploration of tragic affect and thought in Simone Weil, a writer whose sternness is especially vivid and in whom tragic sense and literary sensibility can be seen to embrace. Weil defined the truth as categorically severe, and her sense of this ineluctable severity was clearly intrinsicated with her experience of literature. Her sternness of thought owed something to her affection for Greek tragedy and for Aeschylus in particular. To put it plainly, she expresses her respect and nostalgia for these literary loves by means of her severity. Her case exemplifies the operations of the tragic paradigm, and so it is with her that I begin.

CHAPTER 1

Weil and Aeschylus

Herself a writer of some austerity, Weil thought that the truth stands apart, posing a stern challenge to the complacencies of this world, taking the side of the outcast, despairing, and disenfranchised. The concept of the outcast, or preterite, in Weil's writing is not only an ecclesiastical concept but also a more broadly religious and finally a political one. Sufferers, workers, and "ordinary people" are numbered among the preterite, whose life constitutes a kind of silent tradition without authority. In a letter explaining why she refused to be baptized, Weil wrote to her priest, "Mais à mes yeux le christianisme est catholique en droit et non en fait. Tant de choses sont hors de lui, tant de choses que j'aime et ne veux pas abandonner, tant de choses que Dieu aime, car autrement elles se seraient sans existence.... Je reste aux côtés de toutes les choses qui ne peuvent pas entrer dans l'Eglise" (*Attente* 52, 55). As far as Weil was concerned, the only voice that speaks for this silent world of preterition is literature. The importance of literature lies in its coincidence with "les choses que j'aime et ne veux pas abandonner."[1]

Weil believed, in other words, that literature speaks the truth—just that truth which the world strives to ignore—without mediation, distraction, or interference from its own media. Truth springs forth from the depths in the voice of books. This view of literature as profoundly mimetic Weil maintained steadfastly, with a franker and more intense conviction than any literary critic, including Johnson, would condone. She said outright that "the most beautiful poetry is the poetry which can best express, in its truth, the life of people who can't write poetry" (*Seventy Letters* 104). And she did not hesitate to interpret "the most beautiful poetry" in this light. After working for a year in a Renault factory, she wrote an essay on *Antigone* for her fellow workers. It begins by dismissing the academic and cultural authority of literature in favor of a different kind of authority (if it can still be called that), the authority of being intimate with suffering. "In Greece, almost two thousand five hundred years ago, some very beautiful poems were written. They are scarcely read any longer except by people who specialize in their study, and that is a great misfortune. For these old poems are so human that they are still very close to us and could interest every one. Indeed, they would be much more moving for ordinary people, who know what it is to struggle and to suffer, than for people who have passed their lives between the four walls of a library" (*La Source Grecque* 57). Dismissing the elite academic status of *Antigone*, Weil reserves the play for a more profound role as the friend and comfort of humility. This fierce idealization becomes even bolder when she considers *King Lear*. Quoting Lear's plaint, "Why should a dog, a horse, a cat have life, / And thou no breath at all?", she immediately identifies his words with the voice of the dispossessed: "Helplessness—I do not mean weakness of character, but utter lack of material force—breathes forth in these lines in all its bitterness. For it is bitter; nothing in the world is so bitter. Yet it is better for the soul than triumph and power, because there is truth in it: it is not, like these, poisoned with delusions and lies" (*Seventy Letters* 104). Weil treats Lear's lines, and the emotion expressed in them, as purely and simply identical with the bitterness of suffering whose extremity has brought the knowledge of the "truth."

It is striking that the truth Weil imagines literature to express should take this tragic form—truth purchased at the cost of suffering and helplessness. But indeed, she treats the "truth" of literature as synonymous with what was to her the only deep truth, that which comes from dispossession, loss, and solitude, the knowledge of the world's emptiness and God's absence. This was the experience of "the void," the "dark night of the soul," which grants the necessary knowledge of irredeemable loss. It is the time that "has to be gone through without any reward, natural or supernatural" (*Gravity* 56).

Weil's association of literature with the bitterness of tragic knowledge becomes particularly vivid in a late letter in which she suddenly and passionately launches the claim that "in Shakespeare the fools are the only people who tell the truth":

> When I saw *Lear* here, I asked myself how it was possible that the unbearably tragic character of these fools had not been obvious long ago to everyone, including myself. The tragedy is not the sentimental one it is sometimes thought to be; it is this:
>
> There is a class of people in this world who have fallen into the lowest degree of humiliation, far below beggary, and who are deprived not only of all social consideration but also, in everybody's opinion, of the specific human dignity, reason itself—and these are the only people who, in fact, are able to tell the truth. All the others lie.
>
> In *Lear* it is striking. Even Kent and Cordelia attenuate, mitigate, soften, and veil the truth; and unless they are forced to choose between it and telling a downright lie, they manoeuvre to evade it. (*Seventy Letters* 200)

Shakespeare's play is cast as the transparent medium for these "fools" of truth, whom no one has ever heeded:

> What makes the tragedy extreme is the fact that because the fools possess no academic titles or episcopal dignities and because no one is aware that their sayings deserve the slightest attention—everybody being convinced *a priori* of the contrary, since they are fools—their expression of the truth is not even listened to. Everybody, including Shakespeare's readers and audiences for four centuries, is unaware that what they say is true. And not satirically or humorously true, but simply the truth. Pure unadulterated truth—luminous, profound and essential. (*Seventy Letters* 200)

Weil carries to a feverish pitch Johnson's claim that "truth is, indeed, not often welcome for its own sake" and that "it is scarcely to be heard but from those from whom it can serve no interest to conceal it." If literature, in its strange, haunting relentlessness, is conceived to speak the deep truth, then that truth will necessarily seem challenging, antagonistic, and lonely. Weil goes so far as to say that for four centuries no one but she has heard the truth expressed in *Lear*. No one hears the fools' truth, and no one pays attention to Shakespeare's play, just as, in Weil's philosophy more generally, no one heeds the invisible classes of the outcast, though they are for this reason closer to divinity: "Les paysans, les ourvriers possèdent cette proximité de Dieu, d'une saveur incomparable, qui gît au fond de la pauvreté, de l'absence de considération sociale, et des souffrances longues et lentes" (*Attente* 96).

Because Weil identified her great tenderness for certain literary works with her commitment to the outcasts of society and the preterites of the Church, she felt the same fierce respect for the works of her private canon as for the suffering of "un malheureux." The essay in which this last quotation appears, "Réflexions sur le bon usage des études scolaires en vue de l'Amour de Dieu," argues that intellectual work is the training ground for compassionate faith, not because one learns morality from what one studies, but because one learns how to attend to the invisible from the concentration of studying itself. Here the alignment of books with the outcast becomes eerily direct; or, to be more precise, here the privileged position of literature with respect to suffering is reinvented with unusually pure idealization: "Ainsi il est vrai, quoique paradoxal, qu'une version latine, un problème de gèomètrie, même si on les a manqués, pourvu seulement qu'on leur ait accordé l'espèce d'effort qui convient, peuvent rendre mieux capable un jour, plus tard, si l'occasion s'en présente, de porter à un malheureux, à l'instant de sa suprême détresse, exactement le secours susceptible de le sauver" (*Attente* 97).

The relevance of literature, and in particular its ethical and political relevance, has never been less mediated than it is here. Weil's philosophical and religious thought developed in such close relation to her reading that she associated the suffering of the outcast, one of her loftiest concerns, with the darkness of tragic literature. She maintained a private canon, consisting primarily of the *Iliad, King Lear,* Plato, and Greek tragedy—but it was in Aeschylus that she found the passage most evocative of her convictions. Her treatment of Aeschylus illuminates the means and the end of conflating truth with tragic art.

Weil found the dark truth that literature has to tell distilled in one particular moment in Aeschylus. This moment concerns "the work of the memory of pain," as described by the chastened chorus of *Agamemnon*. This "mémoire doleureuse" is tragic knowledge, the traumatic lesson of fate by which we become convinced of the truth's cruelty:

> He who frankly sings the song of victory for Zeus,
> sings the whole truth of the mind.
>
> For Zeus, who put mortals on the way to wisdom
> who laid it down that learning is suffering,
> though the industrious memory of pain still drips
> before the heart in sleep.
> And to us who are unwilling,
> wisdom of temperance comes.
> From the great throne of the daimons,
> in violence, this favor comes.
>
> (174–83)[2]

Weil read this passage as a direct expression of mystical truth, identical with the truth known by the outcast and suffering, the inarticulate and unheeded. Her conflation of loves—of literature, of truth and justice—motivates the breathtaking assimilations of her gloss on this Aeschylean lyric. The sad and tragic "memory" that drips unceasingly before the heart blossoms in significance until it becomes synonymous with what Weil took to be the profoundest models of truth: "La 'mémoire douloureuse' est la réminiscence de Platon, le souvenir de ce que l'âme a vu quand elle était de l'autre côté du ciel; cette mémoire douloureuse qui se distille dans le sommeil, c'est la 'nuit obscure' de Saint Jean de la Croix" (*La Source Grecque* 45).

Weil was clearly attracted to the severity of Aeschylus' "archaic worldview," with its stern rejection of hubris and humanism and its unsentimental representation of irredeemable misery. As an aphorist of considerable intensity herself, she must also have been drawn to the fierce concision of Aeschylus' poetics. Though she often praised Sophocles for his portrayal of suffering, it was in Aeschylus that she found a passage by means of which to evoke the grim, cruel, gnostic otherworldliness of the truth that she imagined preterition and suffering to harbor. But it was precisely Aeschylus' poetics, rather than empathy or politics, that made him intense enough for her. Weil arrived at her cherished models of the deep truth—the vision from the other world, dark night of the soul, labor and memory of pain—by way of her education in the severities of Greek literature. She then found that literature corresponded with those elements of the world in which she had developed an interest originally when spurred to it by something in her literary experience. She translated the sense of truth embodied in tragic literature into the world of political and social problems. This transposition was made possible by the self-occulting love of mimesis, wherein literature is imagined to express a truth that, in fact, it has itself defined as the truth. This confusion is exposed by the eccentricity of Weil's choice: the aspect of Aeschylus with which she wanted to associate the pain of suffering and unhappiness is in fact no mimesis of human life but a poetics of great figural and affective ambition.

Aeschylus' austerity, along with the density of figuration that serves to enhance it, makes manifest a different poetic ambition from that of his fellow Greek dramatists: the ambition to create a chilling, severe, and august presence for language itself as an analogue of the inhuman forces that loom over human life, an analogue of fate. In *The Frogs*, Aristophanes provides a penetrating characterization of what is forceful in Aeschylus' poetry and reveals those of its qualities that are susceptible to being idealized. The cold and haughty character that Aristophanes bestows on Aeschylus actually allegorizes, with a negative valence, those very qualities in his poetry that Aristophanes admired and for which, at the end of *The Frogs,* he crowns Aeschylus with the highest honors and the right to return to life. Aeschylus takes the palm not only for the beauty of his poetry but for his capacity, as deduced from this beauty, to articulate philosophical truth. So deep is his relationship to the truth that his authority extends over practical and political life: Dionysus brings him back from the dead to guide Athens through a time of civic and military crisis. Thus he is exalted over the philosopher Socrates because tragedy is found to be the superior form of philosophy. Singing his praise, the chorus contends, "Blessed be the man who has xunesin"; in the words of a nineteenth-century definition, "xunesin" is "intelligence made accurate and deep by the study of life" (*Ranae* 135).

> Blessed be he
> who has such wisdom and wit
> Many can learn from it.
> Through good counsel he won the right
> to return home again
> for the good of the cause and state,
> for the good of his fellow men,
> to help him fight the good fight
> with his great brain.
> Better not to sit at the feet
> of Sokrates and chatter,
> nor cast out of the heart
> the high serious matter
> of tragic art.
> (1482–95; *The Frogs* 581–82)

Here "wisdom" is allied to "tragic art." Aeschylus can claim the merit of "high seriousness," profundity and insight, precisely because he is a writer of tragedies, not merely a philosopher; and real understanding, it is implied, resides in the tragic sense. "Tragic art" is thus idealized, invested with a privileged relation to truth and a unique truth-telling capacity. In this form of literary idealization, aesthetic power is identified with, or rather confused with, cognitive success. It is this confusion I mean to isolate under the name "the love of mimesis": love of literature, or response to literary power, that issues in a claim for literature's representational—that is, cognitive or epistemological—authority.

But why does Aristophanes find superior gravity and truthfulness in the tragedies of Aeschylus? In other words, what is it about Aeschylus' plays that make him seem the master of tragic art rather than the other Greek tragedians? In a suggestive though rather dense scene, Aristophanes contrasts the poetics of Euripides and Aeschylus; the scene ends by demonstrating Aeschylus' ascendancy. A competition is staged between the two playwrights, a literalizing and surreal exercise called "the weighing of the lines," in which each puts a sample of his lyrics on an imaginary pair of balance scales to see whose has "the true weight." "Weight" here means aesthetic power, and this power is measured in affective resonance. The "true weight" turns out to be tragic affect, but it is tragedy in a particular sense: Euripidean pathos is found to be weak by contrast to the chilling impersonality and fatalism of Aeschylus.

> Euripides [quoting himself]: "There is no temple for persuasion apart from words."
> Aeschylus: "Death alone of all the gods is not moved by gifts" [Monos theon gap Thanatos ou dopon erai].
> Dionysus: "Let it go, let it go. Aeschylus has the weight again. For he put in Death, heaviest of evils" [Thanaton gar eisentheke barutaton kakon]. (*Ranae* 1391–94)

This exchange is impressively economical in its characterization of Aeschylean poetics; the use of the balance scale and the metaphor of weight manage to suggest that there is something almost material about the grimness of Aeschylus' poetry. Aeschylus wins because he "put death in, heaviest of evils." Naturally, Aeschylus' language of death seems graver than Euripides' language of persuasion, since death is the graver subject. Yet the tropes of heaviness, materiality, and measurement imply that there is a unique influence in the style itself. As Dionysus' judgment suggests ("He put death in"), Aeschylus' poetry seems to make use of what de Man calls "the materiality of the letter"; it offers up the word "thanatos" like a thing—a stone, or a god. This implication is clearer in the Greek, where "thanatos," the direct object, comes first in Dionysus' sentence, an emphasis that calls attention to the word's autonomy. "Thanatos" takes on a certain blankness or opacity, like that of the abstract, impersonal "Death" to which it refers, a feature of life not experienced in its entirety by human subjects. The affect of the poetry thus arises from features of the poetics itself as well as from the representational content of the words. That is not an unusual phenomenon, but in this case, the slightly disorienting or uncanny presence of stylistic effect works thematically to evoke the uncanniness of the personification, Death, and its dreadfulness. The not-quite-mimetic affect of the poetry gives resonance to eerily not-quite-human experience.

The heavier weight of Aeschylus' line comes from the density and severity of its poetics. This poetry is notorious for its difficulty—for being formal, hieratic, and thickly figurative. The ambitions represented by these qualities are antithetical to those of Euripides, in his aim to humanize tragedy and naturalize its language. It seems to be for this reason exactly that Aristophanes finds Aeschylus' poetry the more impressive: it pursues and succeeds at what Aristophanes takes to be more purely literary ambitions—or, rather, ambitions better suited to the unique capacities of literature. "Death" was "put in" to make the weight—that is, to accommodate the poetry's aspiration after power, and specifically after the force of grimness. That aspiration exists for its own sake: the sense of fatality, the "heaviness" or gloom of Aeschylean poetry, is autotelic. To achieve the affect is the first priority; subjects, characters, themes—the objects of mimetic representation—serve as the means to generate the affect. Such, I propose, are the insights embodied in Aristophanes' strange image of "weighing the lines."

Aeschylus' plays work out a poetics that is powerful though not by way of empathic pathos. Poetic language makes its alliance with fatality rather than subjectivity, by participating in the impassivity and impersonality of fate. People, for example, turn into creatures and things, which is how fate sees them. Persian sailors drowning off the coast of Salamis are reduced to dumb physicality: "Like tunny-fish, or like some school to be caught in the net, / They struck against shards of oars, and fragments of the wreck" (*The Persae* 424–26). Humanity loses its contours. At their most passionate, Menelaus and Agamemnon, leaving for Troy, change their throats to the throats of birds:

> ... fiercely shouting the war-cry
> like eagles who in unappeasable grief
> for their offspring,
> wheel
> high above the nest,
> rowing their feathered oars.
> (*Agamemnon* 47–52)

In their emotion, they have become creaturely and remote. But the victims of their rage, the survivors languishing in the ruins of Troy, are objectified by fate through their reification in slavery: "They fall to clasp the bodies of their husbands and brothers; children fall on the aged who begot them. They are bewailing the death of their dearest, from lips that will never be free" (*Agamemnon* 326–29). Here the perspective of fate, with its transformations, is realized in a grand perspective that superimposes different times: these survivors are still technically free, but the verse calls upon us to see them as shadowed by their impending enslavement. Johnson called for such an imperial perspective in the opening lines of "The Vanity of Human Wishes": "Let observation with extensive view / Survey mankind from China to Peru." His aim is clearly superhuman: no one can have so wide a view of space and time. Yet the wide "survey" represents a persistent intellectual dream. It is synonymous with the generalizing overview that provides a common intellectual goal (the one whose seductions Wittgenstein vigorously protested). For the sense of fate and of fatefulness cannot be created without it—that is, without the tropes of generality and impersonality. Thus Aeschylus' cool style tranquilly perceives the continuing fates of subjects who are themselves past experiencing: the corpses of Polynices and Eteocles, who have killed each other in a dispute over their patrimony, lie ready for burial, but "beneath their bodies the richness of earth shall fall down to infinity" (*Seven Against Thebes* 949–50).

Aeschylus' poetry here takes the side of earth, opulent, deathly, and impersonal. Its relentless figural industry provides an affect—the chill of the impersonality of language—for the phenomenon of fatality, which it aims to make manifest. This trait of Greek tragedy—the impassive opulence of figuration—Johnson imitated in his own lines about Xerxes (protagonist of *The Persae*). They were, in fact, his favorite lines from "The Vanity of Human Wishes": "A single skiff to speed his flight remains; / Th' incumber'd oar scarce leaves the dreaded coast / Through purple billows and a floating host" (238–40). But where Johnson has given this figural richness an ironic and moralizing tint, it has none in Aeschylus. His daimonized and industrious poetics simply yields up the voice of an impersonal, malevolent necessity. We might call it Ate, fatality separated from subjectivity and character—fatality as an isolated and personified force but also fatality unmoved by and unconcerned with individual experience.

In his book on Aeschylus, John Herrington suggests that drama in Western culture was essentially shaped by the innovations of Sophocles, which by consequence seemed to render obsolete the "archaic worldview" of Sophocles' monumental predecessor. The new drama eagerly devoted itself to the representation of human subjectivity: "Sophocles and the majority of dramatists who followed him for many centuries tended to focus their plays on clearly outlined and defined individuals, visible onstage. In the growing revelation of those individuals' characters through speech and action, in the interplay of their wills and passions, in the mounting suspense as to the outcome, in the denouement that finally determined their nature and their fates, lay—and lies the fascination of that dramatic mode" (12). By contrast to this drama of human feeling, Aeschylus' austere fatalism, combined so strangely with his linguistic wildness, fell into the dark inaccessibility of the "archaic."

But it is rather as if Aeschylus, instead of simply antedating the representation of character, had determined to abjure its rich fascinations. Whatever the flaws of his dramatis personae—however flamboyant their innocence, hubris, and cruelty—their flaws are not tragic in the sense of precipitating catastrophe. Instead, these characters fall prey to prescribed destruction, to a spirit of fatality that is variously called Alastor (Vengeance), Arai (Curses), Erinyes (Furies), Moira (Doom), and Ate (Madness and Death). The "ruling passion" of the protagonists is generally the expression, the force, of the spirit or spirits that possess them (Cassandra) or haunt them (Orestes) or both, since these forces are able to move freely from interiorized to exteriorized states. Moreover, they command both the literal and the figural aspects of the plays' language, exerting a kind of hegemony over signification. In *Agamemnon,* for example, the "net of necessity" enters the play as a figure for the Greeks' siege of Troy—"over the towers of Troy you threw the close-weaved net of the slavery of Ate, which destroys everyone" (357–62)—and ends by materializing as the robe in which Clytemnestra and Aegisthus entangle Agamemnon, kill him, and enshroud his body.

The "pity and terror" of Aeschylus' plays do not arise from the suffering of individualized characters, since Ate consumes individuality. It might be more accurate to say, in fact, that the possessions and visitations of these metamorphic forces make manifest the insubstantiality of character. Aeschylus' poetic style, with its high formality and rhetorical sophistication, does not, then, reflect a pedantic ambitiousness or a crude ignorance of psychology. Rather than expressing the characters' emotions, this poetry expresses the thrill of the fate that overwhelms them; it produces the literary affect of Johnsonian "shock" as an analogue of contact with the darkness of fate.[3] The "deinon," the uncanny, in Aeschylus' relentlessly severe poetics, stands in for the uncanniness of Ate.

Strangely, it was Aeschylus' autotelic affect of fatality that Simone Weil picked to represent the "truth" of literature—though she may not have known exactly what she was choosing. She identified the "dark memory of pain" with the experience of the preterite; presumably, the sadness and sternness of Aeschylus' poetry seemed to her to answer the experience of the outcast adequately or at least to corroborate the tone she thought appropriate and wanted to strike herself. But in making this identification, she seems to have been confused: like Aristophanes, she was attracted to the severity in Aeschylus, but that same severity is related to his comparative lack of humanism, which makes him an odd choice of a favorite for her. The stern voice of unbrookable truth is in Aeschylus the voice of fatality, which does not speak for people. So there is something a little incoherent in Weil's choice, and this incoherence gives rise to the appearance of exaggerated enthusiasm, misprision, or idealization in her discussion of Aeschylus. She seems to have conflated an achievement of literary language with an empathic moral project.

Weil came to this identification through the respect that she shared with Aeschylus for the category of fate. Pain, memory, and the dark night of the soul are all other names for that fragility of life, that subjection to fate, which Weil took to be to be the most serious of moral facts. For paradoxically, it produces what Weil called "the beauty of the world." We pity the fragility of life, which has fallen victim to fate's severity; and it is this fragility that gives the world beauty in our eyes. Clearly, its beauty will be haunted and tragic—a memento of its imperfection—and that is exactly what makes it valuable to Weil. Material necessity, imbued with the sadness of the absence of God, by a familiar metonymic slide becomes in itself an object of estranged but loving meditation—"Nous sommes avertis de cette part [que la matière] mérite à notre amour par la beauté du monde. Dans la beauté du monde la nécessité brute devient objet d'amour." This passage comes from the essay entitled "L'Amour de Dieu et le malheur"; Weil goes on to make clear what we might have deduced, that the apprehension of "la beauté du monde" is saturated with the affect of mourning. The beauty of the world calls upon us to love material reality as we would the abandoned possessions of one whom we have lost: "Par sa parfaite obéissance la matière mérite d'etre aimée par ceux qui aiment son Maître, comme un amant regarde avec tendresse l'aiguille qui a été maniée par une femme aimée et morte" (*Attente* 112). This association with mourning naturally renders "the beauty of the world" a highly ambivalent phenomenon in the sense that it exalts the world and exposes its poverty at the same time.

A similar process of exaltation and disappointment has been identified in the ideology of the sublime.[4] Weil's thinking seems to have been unconsciously involved with notions of the sublime, especially the literary sublime. It is clear, for example, that her fascination with Aeschylus' lyric on "the memory of pain" and her choice of the other works in her private canon betray an attraction to the same features of "power," "darkness," and intimidation that characterize Burke's models of sublimity. Indeed, it turns out that Weil's literary values inform her ambivalent concept of "the beauty of the world." The "most beautiful poetry" expresses and distills that necessity which "becomes the object of our love." "Toutes les horreurs qui se produisent en ce monde sont comme les plis imprimés aux vagues par la pesanteur. C'est pourquoi elles enferment une beauté. Parfois un poème, tel que l'*Iliade*, rend cette beauté sensible" (*Attente* 112). Literary representation brings "the beauty of the world" to light; yet it is odd that poetry should be found making sensible reality sensible. This paradox suggests that the "beauty" in "the beauty of the world" comes from a kind of refraction, that it is the sheen in the mirror of mimesis. What makes the stirring tenuousness of the world felt is not the world but its representation, whether because the world takes on the frailty of the medium or because, on the contrary, the representation in its immediacy reveals the inaccessibility of the original. "The beauty of the world" springs from mimesis, or rather, from that tenderness for representation and its objects inspired by the love of mimesis. The beauty of the world must be mourned because it does not belong to the world.

The essential shadowiness, the unreality of the beauty of the world, robs life of its substantiality. It makes a cipher of living. Weil firmly, if somewhat unreflectively, proclaimed such an attenuation in her own existence: "it is literally true that friendship gives to my thought all the life it has, apart from what comes to it from God or from the beauty of the world" (*Reader* 92). Here is the drama of the writer's self-loss, a not uncommon phenomenon (or apprehension, at any rate); we will see varieties of literary self-attenuation in Johnson and Shelley as well. And there are vivid examples in Kafka, as Maurice Blanchot has shown,[5] and in Fitzgerald's "The Crack-Up," where he announces dryly, "I have now at last become a writer only" (83).

Life comes to seem attenuated in this way when it is contrasted to, or seen to be dominated by, its powerful other. We have seen Weil use various names for this other—fate, fatality, the void, death. She regarded the preterite and the outcast—life's powerless others—as ranged with these forces by virtue of their alterity and because, more fundamentally, she regarded the truth for which they stood as antithetical, like all truth. Now the mystery is how she came by this concept of the truth. The only strong other to life still accessible to it is literature, which poses itself as a symmetrical opposite by way of mimesis and thus offers itself as the stage for the appearance of the intangible others—fate, the void, the undesired truth of "fools." And Weil did in fact find in literature the place where all that is denied by the world comes to light. Literary mimesis promises to reveal the truth, but the truth that it reveals and the concept of truth that it fosters will be inflected by the lingering sense of its alterity. The truth will partake of the otherness of literature, and when the truth is defined as other, then it is defined as life's antagonist. The literary style that tries to catch up with this austere concept of truth, that tries to instantiate the severity of the truth and in this way to fulfill the destiny of literature, is an imposing, highly wrought, rhetorically dense style—Aeschylus' style—aspiring after aphoristic force and the authority of the impersonal. It is sometimes identified as the literary sublime. Weil aspired to write in this style herself even as she developed philosophical concepts influenced by the hidden postulates and requirements of this aspiration. Thus she exemplified this style, both in its form—its starkness and severity—and in the ideas and assumptions it advances, when she wrote, "To love the truth means to endure the void, and, as a result, to accept death. Truth is on the side of death" (*Gravity* 56).

CHAPTER 2

Johnson in Mourning

For thou art heavenly, she an empty dream.

Like Weil, Johnson was drawn to the integrity and the clarity of stern generalization. The astringency of Johnson's intellectual attitudes, as well as his prose style, makes it clear how much he implicitly believed in the harshness of the truth. But that he held this belief is in a sense not a new discovery. It has conventionally been understood as a feature of his "skepticism." Johnson's was not a religious or philosophical skepticism, of course, for he piously defended against the former and treated the latter with contempt. It was rather a kind of intellectual skepticism, entailing an inveterate mistrust of appearances—especially comforting and happy ones—and a corresponding assumption that the truth to be uncovered would be "contrary to our wishes" and inclinations. Johnson shares this practice and this assumption with many writers, especially analytical ones: vigilance, tough-mindedness, and doubt seem to us the inevitable concomitants of serious thought. But not every author is haunted by these notions; nor is every author's work organized and dominated by the effort, independent of subject, to keep pace with the demand for severity.

Johnson's resolutely demystifying stance and chilling style served to answer and echo the features of his literary experience: through them he established his fidelity to the sense of truth embodied in tragic literature. This is a counterintuitive claim: it is naturally more common to treat Johnson's tragic sense as a fundamental feature of his intellectual personality—a result either of his experience, his disposition, or his settled belief. It is sometimes related to his religious environment and said to be a manifestation of "Christian pessimism" (by Sachs, for example). In any event, his sadness is usually interpreted as the natural consequence of his depth and intelligence—and also as a sign of it. And there are real advantages in this interpretation: critics who participate in Johnson's tragic sense go on to paraphrase his writing with considerable eloquence and sympathy (see Bate, Watkins, and Wharton). Partly for this reason, Johnson scholars rarely go out of their way to investigate the sources of his obsessive grimness or his determination to reproduce it in his writing.[1]

It was not consciously and rigorously, like Weil, but quietly and instinctively that Johnson conceived of literature as the dark antithesis of life and found in literary experience the simulation of emotions associated with privation, solitude, and the fear of death. He attributed to literature a kind of uncanny power to enforce its mimetic effects (rather than being itself simply mimetic), and he feared that he had fallen prey to this power as a perverse consequence of his devotion to books. Literature competed with and quelled life: such was his secret view, which showed itself in a kind of guilt and sorrow for the world. He expressed his sorrow in the lingering Oedipal mourning that is closely associated with his pervasive melancholy. This mourning for the world and its fragility also colors Weil's concept of "the beauty of the world," as we have seen, though, unlike Weil, Johnson lamented rather than embraced that pathos of living things that literature inspires.

It is well known that Johnson mistrusted "the dangerous prevalence of imagination" (*Rasselas* 150). This mistrust is likely to have influenced his literary criticism, perhaps even in involuntary or unconscious forms. Such apprehension or mistrust seems to be active in two particularly uncompromising interrogations of poetic license—one from the "Life of Cowley" and the other from the "Life of Milton," studies of poets whose political activity and aesthetic practice Johnson had already found reason to think perverse.

Cowley, as it turns out, invented the passion and the woman of his poem "The Mistress." Frivolous as this invention is, it gives Johnson strange pause. He regards Cowley's fabrication as a kind of literary demonology, as the generation of a phantom, but one whose uncertain charm he is willing to evoke in echoes from his dearest authors, Shakespeare, Cervantes, and Pindar (never mind Cowley). To Johnson, the unreality of the Mistress has its own real depth: "The desire of pleasing has in different men produced actions of heroism, and effusions of wit; but it seems as reasonable to appear the champion as the poet of an 'airy nothing,' and to quarrel as to write for what Cowley might have learned from his master Pindar to call the 'dream of a shadow'" (*Lives* 1:5). From this oddly loving invocation of shadows, Johnson moves to warn against their creation and indulgence. He portrays Cowley as a writer who dissipated himself in his fictions, like a daydreamer rioting in fantasy:

> It is surely not difficult, in the solitude of a college, or in the bustle of the world, to find useful studies and serious employment. No man needs to be so burthened with life as to squander it in voluntary dreams of fictitious occurrences. The man that sits down to suppose himself charged with treason or peculation, and heats his mind to an elaborate purgation of his character from crimes which he was never within the possibility of committing, differs only by the infrequency of his folly from him who praises beauty which he never saw, complains of jealousy which he never felt; supposes himself sometimes invited, and sometimes forsaken; fatigues his fancy, and ransacks his memory, for images which may exhibit the gaiety of hope, or the gloominess of despair, and dresses his imaginary Chloris or Phyllis sometimes in flowers fading as her beauty, and sometimes in gems lasting as her virtues.
>
> At Paris, as secretary to Lord Jermin, he was engaged in transacting things of real importance with real men and real women, and at that time did not much employ his thought upon phantoms of gallantry. (*Lives* 1:5)

In one of his *Rambler*s, Johnson gravely and evocatively calls daydreaming "this secret prodigality of being" (no. 89, 4:106). Though the picture of Cowley wreathed in such self-stimulating fantasy is more comic than horrifying, Johnson also strikes some gratuitously ominous notes in this passage. It is tipping the picture toward horror to align Cowley's amorous inventions with paranoid fantasies of criminal and even "treasonous" guilt. Johnson is surprisingly prepared to confuse indulgence in a literary convention with a case of psychosis when he suggests that, like any madman, Cowley lost track of his fiction's unreality and "heated his mind" with the imaginary events of his poetry. He was so far entangled, Johnson implies, that he needed the world to set him free, for at last, the passage concludes with eerie emphasis, "At Paris . . . he was engaged in transacting things of real importance with real men and real women."

What stops one here is not the association of danger and poetry but the extent to which Johnson has forced this association. Displeased to find that "The Mistress" is not autobiography, Johnson devises a different biographical significance for it. But he pursues an uncharacteristic literalism in assuming that Cowley had to have become psychologically involved with his fictions. It is this inappropriately elaborated biographical reading that I find most interesting.

Johnson undertakes such a reading again in a hostile paragraph on Milton, a paragraph whose obstinacy and evasiveness are revealing. Johnson is reflecting on the autobiographical details of the invocations to *Paradise Lost* when he finds opportunity for an episode of antirepublicanism:

> Milton, being now cleared from all effects of his disloyalty, had nothing required from him but the common duty of living in quiet, to be rewarded with the common right of protection: but this, which, when he sculked from the approach of his King, was perhaps more than he hoped, seems not to have satisfied him; for no sooner is he safe than he finds himself in danger, *fallen on evil days and evil tongues, and with darkness and with danger compass'd round.* This darkness, had his eyes been better employed, had undoubtedly deserved compassion: but to add the mention of danger was ungrateful and unjust. He was fallen indeed on *evil days;* the time was come in which regicides could no longer boast their wickedness. But of evil tongues for Milton to complain, required impudence at least equal to his other powers; Milton, whose warmest advocates must allow, that he never spared any asperity of reproach or brutality of insolence. (*Lives* 1:101)

What sarcasm is here leveled against one of the more disarming and gentle passages in Milton! Johnson practices some subtle distortion of Milton's poetry to clear the way for this energetic denunciation or else practices this denunciation in order to distract himself from Milton's poetry. This paragraph misrepresents the tone and emphasis of the invocation to Book Seven. It portrays that lyrical interlude as simply carping on the fantasy of "one just man" and assumes, with strange bitterness, that Milton's investment in this view of himself was absolute and that he reproduced his full mind here in all its unmediated "impudence." This last assumption—that Milton is almost uncomfortably accessible in his poem—shares the biographical literalism of the paragraph on Cowley, just as, in both cases, Johnson seems prepared to show that poetry engages the dangerous prevalence of the narcissistic imagination.

I now wish to look at what Johnson has left out in this perversely irritated reading of Milton's invocation. He has left out its sadness. Bitingly he summons up every term of the famous list—the evil days and evil tongues, darkness and danger—until he comes to the last word, which in Milton turns the spirit around:

> Standing on earth, not rapt above the pole
> More safe I sing with mortal voice, unchanged
> To hoarse or mute, though fallen on evil days,
> On evil days though fallen, and evil tongues:
> In darkness, and with dangers compassed round
> And solitude. . . .
>
> (7:23–28)

This list is so fluid that it is beginning to seem easy until the rhythmic singularity of "And solitude" startles the reader. The word "solitude" itself is surprising, since it is the only one in the series without moral nuance. Milton has his verse interrupt its rehearsal of an aggrandizing fantasy to remember the experience of suffering without grandeur or purpose. In this state, recalled to his separation from the world—all passion, all passivity—Milton can evoke the otherworldly warmth of his Muse: "yet not alone, while thou / Visit'st my slumbers nightly" (28–29).

Johnson chose to ignore this pathos in his account of the second invocation—not that, given the context, he had any use for it; but then, he made the context. He chose to be angry with Milton, as with Cowley, and he facilitated his anger by means of a somewhat awkward biographical fallacy. It is as if he preferred to be angry or, more profoundly, wished to preserve a model of poetry—of poets' relationships to their work and his own relationship to them—in which a response such as anger would be appropriate.[2]

Johnson's loyalty to this model was established early in his career. In his first writing on Milton, he temporarily abandoned the model but, after an uncertain pause, gratefully recovered it. Roughly thirty years before he wrote the "Life of Milton," Johnson lent his support to the efforts of William Lauder, who was, through a not very clever ruse, busy to charge Milton with plagiarism. Lauder had found a Latin translation of *Paradise Lost,* and he interpolated passages from it into some of Milton's known Latin sources; he then passed these off for the originals ("An Essay on Milton's Use and Imitation of the Moderns in His *Paradise Lost,*" 1750). He was detected in short order, but not before Johnson had written Lauder's preface, a mistake he was now forced to undo by writing Lauder's retraction. Johnson offered this revisionist scholar only a distant and tentative concurrence, it is true: his disinterested preface represents the pamphlet as a penetrating source study, not as an exposé. Yet in his willingness to cooperate, Johnson seems to have dallied with a wish fulfillment.

But if Johnson wished to eradicate Milton's authority, he was relieved to reinstate it. Both the preface and the retraction carefully preserve Milton's special status; only in the subtle differences of their figural language do these two essays reveal what stake has been hazarded. Aside from one bow to "this mighty genius," the preface avoids recalling the agency of Milton. "*Paradise Lost,*" "the work," and similar phrases take over as the subjects and objects of Johnson's sentences, as when he pictures the poem's development in silent self-propulsion: "Having thus traced the original of this work, I was naturally induced to continue my search to the collateral relations, which it might be supposed to have contracted, in its progress to maturity" (*Works* 5:269). Here is a difficult interpenetration of anthropomorphic and denaturalizing language; the poem may grow up and marry, but its extension is purely contractual, and its "maturity" as artificial as a bond's. Johnson uses these metaphors from law and, elsewhere, metaphors from architecture to elude the organic model of authorship and composition. A poem engineers itself or is engineered by some remote, anonymous builder. So Johnson's figures imply when he explains that source study aims to provide

> a view of the fabrick gradually rising, perhaps from small beginnings, till its foundation rests in the centre, and its turrets sparkle in the skies; to trace back the structure, through all its varieties, to the simplicity of its first plan; to find what was first projected, whence the scheme was taken, how it was improved, by what assistance it was executed, and from what stores the materials were collected, whether its founder dug them from the quarries of nature, or demolished other buildings to embellish his own. (*Works* 5:268)

In this extended metaphor, literature makes its appearance as a depersonalized artifact, shaped by impassive intervention and far remote from psychological verisimilitude.

From this experiment with an autonomy for literature, Johnson returns to the familiarity of the poets. His retraction restores Milton to authorship and sublimity and paternal dominion, as it restores Johnson to his place in a hierarchy of human relations. This alteration can be seen in the altered configuration of one particular metaphor—the figure of the sun coming out from behind the clouds. In the preface, Milton's poem shakes off its shady author to emerge in independent glory. With this assertion of independence, the essay, like a manifesto, begins, "It is now more than half a century since the Paradise Lost, having broke through the clouds with which the unpopularity of the author, for a time, obscured it, has attracted the general admiration of mankind" (*Works* 5:267). But in the retraction, the metaphor recovers its original Shakespearean configuration, testifying to the invincible sovereignty of Milton, king and father: now, with the detection of Lauder's forgeries, "the shade which began to gather on the splendour of Milton [has been] totally dispersed" (*Works* 5:273). The retraction throughout displays excessive guilt and egregious humility, treating the attack on Milton as an attack on truth and mankind and hastening to reconsolidate Milton's authority by reserving for him the language of monolithic power.

As if the outcome of this crisis motivated the unusual consistency, or conservatism, of his writing, Johnson remained forevermore faithful to this lionization of Milton and to the personalization of literature. It is clear from his interest in biography that he wished above all to sustain the company of the poets. He was for this reason willing to exaggerate occasions for anger, such as the memory of Milton's politics, or his personal failings, or his use of blank verse.³ Johnson is then able to make reparation with tender and remorseful acknowledgments, often staying his regrets until final, sonorous paragraphs. At the end of the "Life of Milton," he transforms Milton's "impudent," self-imposed isolation into heroism and turns his own recalcitrance to mourning:

> But, of all the borrowers from Homer, Milton is perhaps the least indebted. He was naturally a thinker for himself, confident of his own abilities, and disdainful of help or hindrance: he did not refuse admission to the thought or images of his predecessors, but he did not seek them. From his contemporaries he neither courted nor received support; there is in his writings nothing by which the pride of other authors might be gratified, or favour gained; no exchange of praise, nor solicitation of support. His great works were performed under discountenance, and in blindness, but difficulties vanished at his touch; he was born for whatever is arduous; and his work is not the greatest of heroick poems, only because it is not the first. (*Lives* 1:139)

Yet this account of Johnson's fondness for biography does not quite explain why he obscures the pathos of the invocation to Book Seven. In order to explore this problem, I am going to look at another example of the suppression of pathos in the "Life of Milton." Here also Johnson treats a powerful moment in Milton's poetry as if it were mediocre and trivial, little interesting except from a biographical point of view. In an especially brisk paragraph, Johnson summarizes some vicissitudes of Milton's domestic history: "About this time his first wife died in childbed, having left him three daughters. As he probably did not much love her, he did not long continue the appearance of lamenting her; but after a short time married Catherine, the daughter of one Captain Woodcock of

Hackney; a woman doubtless educated in opinions like his own. She died, within a year, of childbirth, or some distemper that followed it; and her husband honored her memory with a poor sonnet" (*Lives* 1:84). It has been a long time since anyone called "Methought I saw my late espoused saint" a poor sonnet. If Johnson was indifferent to the poem, indifferent enough to dismiss it with an almost ostentatious economy, he may have chosen this chill response out of loyalty to a standard more compelling than taste.

Boswell reports what would seem to be a similarly motivated elision in the "Life of Parnell." Parnell was promoted to a vicarage, "but," says Johnson, "his prosperity did not last long. His end, whatever was its cause, was now approaching" (*Lives* 1:397). To produce this disinterested summary, Johnson struck his first and more sonorous version: "But his prosperity was clouded by that which took away all his powers of enjoying either profit or pleasure, the death of his wife, whom he is said to have lamented with such sorrow, as hastened his end" (Boswell 1106). This sentence echoes the famous conclusion of the preface to the *Dictionary:* "I have protracted my work till most of those, whom I wished to please have sunk into the grave, and success and miscarriage are empty sounds" (*Works* 5:51). It is as if Johnson had suppressed the sentence in order to silence the echo of his own words. Boswell is alert to this suppressed resonance, remarking keenly, "I should have thought that Johnson, who had felt the severe affliction from which Parnell never recovered, would have preserved this passage" (1106). Johnson was apparently very unwilling to allow, or acknowledge, such an identification with a widower. (I have found only one example, from a letter written not long after Elizabeth Johnson's death; and even here, Johnson is compassionating a friend, not a poem or a biographical subject.)

Johnson's diaries reveal that he was familiar with the experiences of "Methought I saw my late espoused saint." Yet they also testify to an ambivalence about his mourning that may have helped him to suppress potential identifications. A sermon written for his wife's funeral is peculiarly emphatic about the inaccessibility of the dead; in grief, "the whole mind becomes a gloomy vacuity, without any image or form of pleasure, a chaos of confused wishes, directed to no particular end, or to that which, while we wish, we cannot hope to obtain; for the dead will not revive; those whom God has called away from the present state of existence, can be seen no more in it; we must go to them; but they cannot return to us" (*Sermons* 267). This urgent self-admonishing gave way, and, in a prayer composed a month later, Johnson pleads, "O Lord, Governor of Heaven and Earth, in whose hands are embodied and departed spirits, if thou hast ordained the souls of the dead to minister to the living, and appointed my departed wife to have care of me, grant that I may enjoy the good effects of her attention and ministration, whether exercised by appearance, impulses, dreams, or in any other manner agreeable to thy government" (*Diaries* 46). But the violence of these wishes made him anxious; at the same date, he prays to be preserved from "fruitless grief, or tumultuous imaginations" (*Diaries* 46), and a year later he remains fearful about the teleology of his mourning: "Apr. 29, 1753. I know not whether I do not too much indulge the vain longings of affection; but I hope they intenerate my heart & when I die like my Tetty this affection will be acknowledged in a happy interview & that in the meantime I am incited by it to piety. I will however not deviate too much from common & received methods of devotion" (*Diaries* 53–54). Johnson treats his own grief as dubious and alien, to be suppressed in favor of ceremonies "common and received."

This anxiety about emotional deviation seems to have encouraged Johnson in some linguistic eccentricities. He developed the habit of using abbreviations and foreign phrases to allude to mourning—this in his private papers, which he wrote for his reading alone and many of which he succeeded in destroying just before his death. Here he keeps detailed accounts of his personal mourning rites at the same time that he is driven to euphemism. He reports praying for Tetty in church and wants to confess his emotion, but not without changing languages: "I repeated mentally the commendation of her with the utmost fervour larme à l'oeil before the reception of each element at the altar. I repeated it again in the pew, in the garden before dinner, in the garden before departure, at home at night. I hope I did not sin. Fluunt lacrymae" (*Diaries* 52–53). When he wants to say that he has cried, Johnson flees to foreign phrases, as if there were a language within language where sorrow might be contained. Later in the journal of his prayers, he stops writing the words for death, using the abbreviations "Θ." and "Θ.ϕ." for "dead" and "dead friends" (*Diaries* 259, 296, 329).

It should be remembered that not only Latin and Greek but also French belonged among the dead languages to Johnson: they were his literary languages, confined to reading, writing, and quotation. Their silence no doubt made them attractive to secrecy and euphemism. Johnson hid not only his mourning but his inner life more generally under the cloak of such euphemisms; in 1784 he repented his "μχ. αἰσχ-νο κεσβ," apparently meaning that he had been racked by "melancholy, shameful thoughts," and "vain resolutions" (*Diaries* 378). Johnson allowed his sadness and anxiety to take harbor in dead languages. Without rising to speech, invisible pain transformed itself into their silence. Interestingly enough, the silent experience of reading undergoes the same transformation. In another ambivalently informative note, Johnson adopts Latin when he confesses his vulnerability to literature: [Good Friday, 1765] "Slept ill. Rose. Mr. Lye. To Church at the lesson; heard ill. Graham. Sat at home. Read Nelson, then read Temple. In reading Nelson thought on Death cum lacrimis" (*Diaries* 91).

If Johnson's sadness fled to other languages, it pivoted on them and returned in their literatures. Hester Thrale wrote (bringing us back to the question of Milton's sonnet), "Of the pathetic in poetry he never liked to speak" (Piozzi 129). In spite of this continence, he could not resist Church Latin, for, Thrale goes on, "It was not however from the want of a susceptible heart that he hated to cite tender expressions, for he was more strongly and more violently affected by the force of words representing ideas capable of affecting him at all, than any other man in the world I believe; and when he would try to repeat the celebrated *Prosa Ecclesiastica pro Mortuis,* as it is called, beginning *Dies irae, Dies illa,* he could never pass the stanza ending thus, *Tantus labor non sit cassus* [Let not so much toil be vain], without bursting into a flood of tears" (Piozzi 130). In this account, Thrale candidly shows that what mattered to Johnson was not the sentiment so much as the rhetoric—the texture of spoken signifiers. The "force of words" disarmed him to such an extent that he suppressed them in silence, "never [liking] to speak" of moving poetry and "[hating] to cite tender expressions." But in the silence of writing, he was much more willing to cite, and it is here that Greek and Latin quotations really figure. In that one example of his identification with a widower, Johnson reverts to Euripides under the pressure of distress:

[To Thomas Warton, 21 Dec. 1754] You know poor Mr. Dodsly has lost his Wife, I believe he is much affected. I hope he will not suffer so much as I yet suffer for the loss of mine.
Οἴμι. τι δ᾽οἴμι. Θνῆτα γάρ πεπόνθαμεν.
[Alas! Yet why alas? For we were born to mortal fate.]
I have ever since seemed to myself broken off from mankind a kind of solitary wanderer in the wild of life, without any certain direction, or fixed point of view. A gloomy gazer on a World to which I have little relation. (*Letters* 1:90)

Quoting this passage from Euripides actually seems to make Johnson change the terms of his lament; sympathetic identification yields to a wildly literary language of solitude. It is as if Johnson felt his isolation, his "gloomy gazing," to be bound up with the experience of Greek literature.[4] He may in turn have suppressed this association in Milton's case because Milton wrote in the too-audible words of the living language, English.

It is impressive to find literary pathos among the other phenomena, God and death, that Johnson buried in the silence of great anxiety. If Thrale's remark is to be credited, then Johnson was reluctant to talk about "the pathetic" in public, though he sometimes acknowledged his literary distress in writing. This self-imposed muteness, this silent writing from books to books, dramatically separates literature from what Johnson called "the living world." Yet, along with the rest of his own work, diaries aside, Johnson's writing on pathos is deliberately public, conscious and glad of its audience. It treats pathos as a place of isolating trauma from which one hastens back to the world. In his notes to *Othello,* Johnson finishes his plodding and weary emendations of the murder scene, then startlingly avows, "I am glad that I have ended my revisal of this dreadful scene. It is not to be endured" (*Johnson Shakespeare* 8:1045). Johnson writes as if the encrypted horror of the scene were closing over behind him and he were once again free to speak amid human company. This flight to "the living world" seems still more dramatic in his famous remarks on the death of Cordelia. Only under the canopy of the public opinion will Johnson divulge his pain at reading *Lear:* "And, if my sensations could add any thing to the general suffrage,

I might relate, that I was many years ago so shocked by Cordelia's death, that I know not whether I ever endured to read again the last scenes of the play till I undertook to revise them as an editor." (*Johnson Shakespeare* 8:704). This admission, it will be remembered, appears in defense of Tate's *Lear,* which Johnson seriously favored. His preference for Tate makes it clear that by "shock" he meant something less refreshing than the "pleasures of tragedy" that his contemporaries so admired.

Johnson's concern about the secret inhumanity of literature appears, here and elsewhere, in his exaggerated reconstitution of the difference between books and "the living world." This difference, in turn, he exemplified in his critical portraits of antiquarians, scientists, and scholars, whom he liked to represent as dusty and spectral. An Oxford fellow whom he had known in their shared youth he dismissed for being now "lost in a convent's solitary gloom" (Boswell 191). He favored such figures of immersion and attenuation in his pejorative remarks on book-learning. In a *Rambler* that Johnson's nineteenth-century editor called "the study of life not to be neglected for the sake of books" (a superfluous command, one would think), he characterizes "the scholastic race" as "men bred in shades and silence" (no. 180, 5:184). This Gothic vocabulary yields to still more unsavory language in another *Rambler* in which a former scholar confesses that he abandoned his studies when he found his mind "contracted and stiffened by solitude." His grave degeneration led to departures from companionability, a fault that, says the ex-student, "I soon discovered to be one of those intellectual diseases which a wise man should make haste to cure. I therefore resolved for a time to shut my books, and learn again the art of conversation; to defecate and clear my mind by brisker motions and stronger impulses; and to unite myself once more to the living generation" (no. 177, 5:169). In keeping with the metaphor of disease, this passage describes the experience of the mind in highly palpable terms drawn from the experience of the body ("contracted," "stiffened," "defecate and clear," "brisker motions," "stronger impulses"). With this too-vivid language, a contagious desiccation seems to creep from the student's books into his mind. The hidden figure of metastasis—the metastasis of death, in fact—gives a special resonance to the student's resolve that he will "unite [himself] once more to the living generation."

This touch of the macabre is typical of the defensive distaste with which the *Rambler* chides pedantry. Yet its dread of an encroaching, papery lifelessness is not entirely authentic. With the motif of the arid pedant, Johnson misrepresents his anxiety about the effects of literary experience. Such moments are meant not to portray any real "danger" of scholarship so much as they are designed to evoke the pathos of "the living world." In the character of Gelidus, the frozen scholar, Johnson invents a solipsist to chastise for being "unqualified to perform those offices by which the concatenation of society is preserved, and mutual tenderness excited and maintained" (no. 24, 3:132). This figure is so absorbed in treatises and calculations that he has arrived at a zombie's self-sufficiency: "He spends his time in the highest room of his house, into which none of his family are suffered to enter; and when he comes down to his dinner, or his rest, he walks about like a stranger that is there only for a day, without any tokens of regard or tenderness. He has totally divested himself of all human sensations" (3:132–33). What faint drollery there is in this description disappears when Johnson reaches his end, the sudden heightening of pathos with the return of the "living generation": "Thus lives this great philosopher, insensible to every spectacle of distress, and unmoved by the loudest call of social nature, for want of considering that men are designed for the succour and comfort of each other" (3:133). Gelidus, the figure of such perfect, "unmoved" insensibility, is clearly a straw man whom Johnson conjures up and dismisses on his way to something else. What seems to draw him here is the imperative to evoke sadness and apprehension for the fragility of people in their interdependence.

Johnson tends to represent "the living world" this way—as if it were cast into darkness by some unseen spirit of antagonism. The living world then turns out to be as much a tenuous shadow as it is a warm and vigorous presence. Johnson appears to have been riveted by this trope of the pathos of the living. In his letters, he writes such plaintively urgent reminders as "I think it time that we should see one another, and spend a little of our short life together" (*Letters* 1:254), or "We that have lived to lose many that might have cared for us, should care a little for one another" (2:22), or "When I see her again, how I shall love her. If we could keep a while longer together, we should all, I hope, try to be thankful" (2:22). Why does Johnson's living world gather up such acute pathos? This poignancy indicates a superaddition of affect, a diversion of pathos from another place. The trope appears to precede its rationale: the rationale would be the immanence of death, a fit candidate for the role of "unseen antagonist," but I am suggesting that existential affects such as the fear of death are, here at least, derived and secondary in Johnson. With Gelidus as its representative, the antagonist of the living world is that which has no affect but remains "insensible" and "unmoved." Yet Gelidus seems to be a false antagonist.

To illuminate the real nature of Johnson's anxiety, let me turn to another passage on the pathos of the living world. Johnson's *Rambler* on Suspirius, the gloomy prophet of "evil," ends by resuscitating the solemn duties of society:

> To hear complaints with patience, even when complaints are vain, is one of the duties of friendship; and though it must be allowed that he suffers most like a hero that hides his grief in silence . . . yet it cannot be denied, that he who complains acts like a man, like a social being, who looks for help from his fellow creatures. Pity is to many of the unhappy a source of comfort in hopeless distresses, as it contributes to recommend them to themselves, by proving that they have not lost the regard of others; and heaven seems to indicate the duty even of barren compassion, by inclining us to weep for evils which we cannot remedy. (no. 59, 3:318)

Johnson here describes two inverse phenomena—the heroism of grief hidden in silence and the humanity of compassion stirred, though in vain. What would it do to the solemn pathos of this sentiment to remember the shadows of these phenomena in literary experience—imaginary grief consigned to silence and compassion made barren without human objects?

It seems that Johnson felt constrained to protect the living world against the dubious legitimacy of literary experience. If we return to his remarks on the death of Cordelia, we will see this constraint in operation. Here Johnson softens the requirements of mimesis in deference to the audience's susceptibility: "A play in which the wicked prosper, and the virtuous miscarry, may doubtless be good, because it is a just representation of the common events of human life: but since all reasonable beings naturally love justice, I cannot easily be persuaded, that the observation of justice makes a play worse; or, that if other excellencies are equal, the audience will not always rise better pleased from the final triumph of persecuted virtue" (*Johnson Shakespeare* 8:704). If all other excellencies are equal, a literary work should yield to the wishes of its audience's love, pleasure, and peace. This paradigm allows for a surprising redistribution of strength and vulnerability. Literature does not call for sensitive treatment; on the contrary, here it is the play's freedom to be relentless and the audience's weakness to need accommodation. Such a paradigm hints at literature's temptation to the perverse and thus illuminates what is "so shocking" in the death of Cordelia. Earlier in his discussion, Johnson had begun to wonder at the play's "strangeness": "Shakespeare has suffered the virtue of Cordelia to perish in a just cause, contrary to the natural ideas of justice, to the hope of the reader, and, what is yet more strange, to the faith of chronicles" (*Johnson Shakespeare* 8:704). With gratuitous and inventive cruelty, the play propagates a death whose only end is its "shock" to the audience. This perversity could be called malice if it had a human author, but since Johnson is careful to treat the play as impersonal and impassive, its painful affect seems to be born ex nihilo.

Yet that pain could still count as part of the living world, as a lawful response to the painful representation of Cordelia's death. In other critical works, Johnson discovers phantom suffering that is stimulated by literature, not as a representation of life but only as an insensible artifact. In these cases, the phantom suffering is acute enough, though not the same as the affect of pathos. The improvident Richard Savage grew passionately solicitous about his galley proofs, agonizing over the punctuation, revising and restoring so often that Johnson calls him "dubious and irresolute without end, as on a question of the last importance" (*Lives* 2:131). Turning to more dramatic language, Johnson expatiates, "The intrusion or omission of a comma was sufficient to discompose him, and he would lament an error of a single letter as a heavy calamity. In one of his letters relating to an impression of some verses, he remarks, that he had, with regard to the correction of the proof, 'a spell upon him'; and indeed the anxiety with which he dwelt upon the minutest and most trifling niceties, deserved no other name than that of fascination" (*Lives* 2:131). Despite some rueful humor, this passage worries the asymmetry between Savage's affects and their object: out of the most trivial and superficial features of literature is born an impressive turbulence of the interior—doubt, agitation, lament, anxiety, obsession.5 Here and in the case of other writers Johnson exemplifies the phenomenon of phantom suffering as an obscurely fatal enthrallment to the foibles of the signifier. Cowley was attracted to silly puns and conceits "by some fascination not easily surmounted" or even "by a kind of destiny" (*Lives* 1:38). But Johnson reserves a more poignant language of tragic infatuation for Shakespeare himself: "A quibble is to Shakespeare, what luminous vapours are to the traveller; he follows it at all adventures, it is sure to lead him out of his way, and sure to engulf him in the mire. It has some malignant power over his mind, and its fascinations are irresistible. . . . A quibble, poor and barren as it is, gave him such delight, that he was content to purchase it, by the sacrifice of reason, propriety and truth. A quibble was to him the fatal Cleopatra for which he lost the world, and was content to lose it" (*Johnson Shakespeare* 7:74). It is odd to characterize punning as a suicidal passion. To make it look so, Johnson portrays the quibble as an autonomous thing, an eerie phantom that Shakespeare pursues in the ignis fatuus. Through this invention, Johnson conjures up a tragic interiority that has accumulated in response to the insubstantial and elusive surfaces of representation.

Johnson described a similar syndrome in the reader of *Paradise Lost*, a syndrome of distress, that is, that arises from having experience with literature though not precisely from being moved by it. In a famous remark, he assures us that *Paradise Lost* wants "human interest," but this, which amounts to the absence of "the pathetic," does not prevent the poem from becoming a source of pain: "But original deficience cannot be supplied. The want of human interest is always felt. *Paradise Lost* is one of the books which the reader admires and lays down, and forgets to take up again. None ever wished it longer than it is. Its perusal is a duty rather than a pleasure. We read Milton for instruction, retire harassed and overburdened, and look elsewhere for recreation; we desert our master and seek for companions" (*Lives* 1:132).

This passage slides precipitously from a criticism of blank "deficience" into a drama of indolence, anxiety, and guilt, mental torments that are familiar from the *Rambler* or from Johnson's own *Prayers and Meditations*. The reader begins with boredom, progresses to gloomy obligation, and concludes "harassed and overburdened," fleeing from the poem's harsh solitude to the comforts of "the living world." This unhappiness does not echo any pathos in *Paradise Lost* but emerges out of its blankness, like Shakespeare's fatal "fascination" with puns.

In his theoretical account of literary affect and literary identification, Johnson does fleetingly envision the stimulation of a spurious interiority. He pauses in his essay on Shakespeare to consider the question of "how the drama moves, if it is not credited" (*Johnson Shakespeare* 7:78). The direct communication of affect is the issue here, and Johnson at first explains it in conventional terms, as the effect of a proleptic identification experienced at a safe distance: "[The drama] is credited, whenever it moves, as a just picture of a real original; as representing to the auditor what he would himself feel, if he were to do or suffer what is there feigned to be suffered or to be done. The reflection that strikes the heart is not, that the evils before us are real evils, but that they are evils to which we ourselves may be exposed." But at this point, Johnson swerves away from the old saw to intimate the decay of that safe distance in a more perfect and literal incorporation of fictional affects: "If there be any fallacy, it is not that we fancy the players, but that we fancy ourselves unhappy for a moment" (*Johnson Shakespeare* 7:78).

Here the security of prolepsis and the externality of representation disappear; instead of congratulating ourselves on our freedom from the characters' woes, "we fancy ourselves unhappy for a moment." Fictional unhappiness has been made real. (It remains to be seen how the qualification "for a moment" will hold up.) Johnson now retreats from this implication, adding, "but we rather lament the possibility than suppose the presence of misery" (*Johnson Shakespeare* 7:78). What is signified in the transition from "fancying" ourselves unhappy to "lamenting the possibility" of unhappiness? The affect may be slightly different (though "lament" bears the traces of "present misery"), yet the process of internalization and realization remains the same. Johnson restores prolepsis, but without the recollection of fictionality. The internalization of spurious and unreal distress proceeds so successfully that its results remind Johnson of the imminence and the dread of death: "We rather lament the possibility than suppose the presence of misery, as a mother weeps over her babe, when she remembers that death may take it from her" (*Johnson Shakespeare* 7:78).

Earlier in the preface to Shakespeare, Johnson makes statements that suggest not only the fatality of literary experience but also its priority to experience of the living world. His familiar argument that Shakespeare wrote from Nature, that he "caught his ideas from the living world" (*Johnson Shakespeare* 7:63), actually works to imply that the autonomy of Nature emerges late in general history and in individual development. It is historically belated, since, after generations of fabulists, Shakespeare was the first English writer to "[show] life in its native colors" (*Johnson Shakespeare* 7:82). Readers before his time had in fact preferred the fabulists because, Johnson strangely affirms, their exposure to literature preceded their acquaintance with Nature, an inevitability that made them as credulous as children: "Nations, like individuals, have their infancy. A people newly awakened to literary curiosity, being yet unacquainted with the true state of things, knows not how to judge of that which is proposed as its resemblance" (*Johnson Shakespeare* 7:82). Here Johnson appears to be treating "literary curiosity" as if it came before the search to know Nature and, in fact, stimulates it, as a means to understanding and evaluating books. Earlier in the preface, when he first exalts Shakespeare's fidelity to Nature and promises its comforts to individual readers, Johnson seems to be following such a chronology, though his use of it there is more troubled as well as more consequential. He is preoccupied with the didactic potential of literature and with its approach to coincidence with life, but his tests for this coincidence always involve isolated people who have come to books first and who sometimes remain isolated among them. The figures in this paragraph apparently live in closets and read in promiscuous solitude: "This therefore is the praise of Shakespeare, that his drama is the mirror of life; that he who has mazed his imagination, in following the phantoms which other writers raise up before him, may here be cured of his delirious extasies, by reading human sentiments in human language; by scenes from which a hermit may estimate the transactions of the world, and a confessor predict the progress of his passions" (*Johnson Shakespeare* 7:65). If a person is to gain his or her knowledge of life through literature, what would be the fate of the confessor and the hermit who were exposed first to the "delirious extasies" of some books and who tried to see the world through them? Johnson even says that writers other than Shakespeare "disguise the most natural passions and most frequent incidents; so that he who contemplates them in the book will not know them in the world" (*Johnson Shakespeare* 7:64–65), as if one's disorientation were experienced, not in reading, but in turning to life. Someone to whom books had come first would be disoriented to find that the world does not coincide with literature but would continue to seek out such a coincidence in order to be relieved from the restless tedium of this disorientation. This seems to have been the case with Johnson, who hunted down occasions for literary gloom, as is suggested by the following letter, with its talk of coincidence and sorrow:

> At Durham, beside all expectation, I met an old friend. . . . I thought her much decayed, and having since heard that the Banker had involved her husband in his extensive ruin, I cannot forbear to think, that I saw in her withered features more impressions of sorrow than of time.
>
> Qua terra patet, fera regnat Erinnys [Where earth extends, there reigns the savage Fury].
>
> He that wanders about the world sees new forms of human misery, and if he chances to meet an old friend, meets a face darkened with troubles. (*Letters* 2:49–50)

The "old friend" whom Johnson comes upon in his wanderings is the quotation from Ovid, which he detects staring out at him from the face of a former acquaintance. Here books do not illuminate life but rather the reverse. In fact, Johnson sometimes allows that the lessons of literature can exercise this peculiar ascendancy. That is the assumption behind his remarks on didacticism and exemplarity, which were familiar concerns of his age but which he seems to have understood more subtly than his contemporaries. He did not, for example, follow the simple model of exemplarity in which an audience at *The Beggar's Opera* leaves the play determined to become highwaymen (Boswell 628–29). His discussions of exemplarity grant to literature a power of influence whose danger lies in its secrecy and silence. Literature stimulates the impulse to imitation, but this imitation occurs without the authority of intention or the check of consciousness.

In the famous *Rambler* no. 4, said to have been occasioned by the popularity of *Roderick Random* and *Tom Jones*, Johnson claims that literary realism is insidious because it is insufficiently tendentious and selective. Its "promiscuous descriptions" become alarming in the light of imitation without authority, whose unseen workings a good author would remember and circumscribe: "But if the power of example is so great, as to take possession of the memory by a kind of violence, and produce effects almost without the intervention of the will, care ought to be taken, that, when the choice is unrestrained, the best examples only should be exhibited; and that which is likely to operate so strongly, should not be mischievous or uncertain in its effects" (3:22). It is hard to imagine how literature might be so well policed as to ensure perfect "certainty" in its effects, and indeed, *Rambler* no. 4 is so anxious about this necessity that it comes to seem considerably more doubtful than confident of literature's moral efficacy. But what I want to concentrate on is the mechanism of its dubious legitimacy—that is, on the power of literary example to "take possession of the memory by a kind of violence" and to "produce effects almost without the intervention of the will." This is a phenomenon of involuntary quotation, but as in Johnson's account of "how the drama moves," it is quotation transformed into interiority, literature echoed in the living world.

In Johnson's works, the image of human authority is already a source of sadness. People who have painfully acquired the authority of knowledge and experience do not gain in power or substance but in isolation and attenuation. To have authority in Johnson is to move in a fainter sphere, as a diminished thing amid insubstantial company. Rasselas best exemplifies the severity of this reverse, when he gives warning to some young bloods: "Let us consider that youth is of no long duration, and that in maturer age, when the enchantments of fancy shall cease, and phantoms of delight dance no more about us, we shall have no comforts but the esteem of wise men, and the means of doing good" (*Rasselas* 69). The great pleasures of the narcissistic imagination do not dwindle into tamer satisfactions but vanish altogether, and in their place rise the small, harsh "comforts" of selfless duty and mild esteem. This is the pathos of authority—to be requited with deprivation, loneliness, and self-loss. Such, Johnson claims, was the disappointment he experienced in the course of compiling his *Dictionary;* at first he thought himself invested with significance and authority, "but these were the dreams of a poet, doomed at last to wake a lexicographer" (*Works* 5:43).

Johnson is willing to stir this pathos even out of Shakespeare's scant biography. Like others, he enjoys the myth of Shakespeare's Adamic freedom, affirming that, unburdened by critics and precursors, he wrote "with the world open before him" (*Johnson Shakespeare* 7:69). But in the course of Johnson's essay, this freedom turns into isolation and neglect. Without authorities to direct or approve him, Shakespeare had to guide himself, in silence and invisibility. A person of his time who wished to study Nature "was under the necessity of gleaning his own remarks, by mingling as he could in [the world's] business and amusements" (*Johnson Shakespeare* 7:88). And such solitary, uncertain research Shakespeare pursued, or so Johnson seems to be thinking when he writes, "Shakespeare must have looked upon mankind with perspicacity, in the highest degree curious and attentive" (*Johnson Shakespeare* 7:88). His power made him more watchful, though perhaps less regarded. Yet as a consequence of his originality, Shakespeare did not value his work but joined his audience in the evanescence of the present: "It does not appear that Shakespeare thought his works worthy of posterity, that he levied any ideal tribute upon future times, or had any further prospect, than of present popularity and present profit. When his plays had been acted, his hope was at an end" (*Johnson Shakespeare* 7:91–92). In Johnson's imagining, the result of Shakespeare's authority was to make him abandon himself. The containment of his hope is especially sobering, since Johnson usually ascribes to hope great ebullience and tenacity. Authority then seems sad to behold, because it exacts the subject's erosion by his or her own advances. The Astronomer of *Rasselas* mourns this fatality, regretting that "I have purchased knowledge at the expense of all the common comforts of life" (*Rasselas* 161).

But despite his fondness for this trope, Johnson saw that the pathos of authority can be sheer fantasy, particularly when it is indulged by the imagination in its tenaciously narcissistic practice. One can easily enough invent and then grieve for one's "lonely wisdom and silent dignity," in the words of an admonishing *Rambler* (no. 135, 4:351). And this is what the mad Astronomer does. It is no less rueful that he should so naturally appropriate, and so pointlessly live out, the pathos of tragic authority than that his madness should have grown out of his "literary solitude" to begin with. With his chimerical burdens and self-imposed isolation, the Astronomer throws his life away on a fantasy of brave, afflicted greatness (or, as he grimly says, "I am . . . tempted to think that my enquiries have ended in errour, and that I have suffered much, and suffered it in vain" [*Rasselas* 161]). To contrast with this narcissistic effulgence, Johnson introduces a depressive "old man" who seems to be the Astronomer's self-mystified double. He is a "sage"—ancient, knowing, and cold. In consequence of his sanity and wisdom, his interest in others and in himself has dwindled to a pip; in fact, his description of his life is so summarily bleak that it angers and debilitates his audience, who were prepared to be moved and instructed by him. Between the Astronomer and the old man, authority makes its last sacrifice, abandoning the pleasures of narcissism, so that now, the old man insists, even praise is to him "an empty sound" (*Rasselas* 155). In the perfection of his clear-sightedness, the sage does not allow himself the comfort of approving his "lonely wisdom and silent dignity" but only lingers on as a body awaiting death. "The transition from the protection of others to our own conduct is a very awful point of human existence," Johnson wrote to a friend (*Letters* 2:199); and it will now be seen how he could view this transition with such sadness. The "empty sounds" that float around the sage recall the "empty sounds" at the end of the preface to the *Dictionary* ("and success and miscarriage are empty sounds"). To have attained the authority of wisdom and experience is to have grown out of the world of people into the world of "empty sounds"—that is to say, into a world that echoes with the involuntary quotations of imitation without authority.

One night at dinner, in the last year of his life, Johnson engaged in a favorite debate on the prevalence of unhappiness. When he was asked how he could be so cheerful in company and yet so obstinate in his affirmations of misery, he explained, "Alas! It is all outside; I may be cracking my joke, and cursing the sun. *Sun, how I hate thy beams!*" (Boswell

1300). Here resurfaces that experience Johnson had suppressed in the "Life of Milton"—that "solitude" of pained interiority and tragic separation from the world. In what are already Shakespearean cadences, the Satan of *Paradise Lost* ranges in his isolation, cursing the stars: "to thee I call, / O sun, to tell thee how I hate thy beams / That bring to my remembrance from what state I fell, / How glorious once above thy sphere" (4:35–39). This is what Johnson produces (though gaily) as the content of his interiority, as if his separation from the world were predicated on the memory and quotation of Milton. I am reminded here of Nicholas Abraham and Maria Torok on a case of endocryptic identification: "It takes some time to understand that he speaks and lives someone else's words and affects." In "A Poetics of Psychoanalysis: 'The Lost Object—Me,'" Abraham and Torok describe this phenomenon as a denial of mourning, a secret incorporation of a lost loved object that allows you to miss yourself in their place. This secret, necessarily inventive incorporation makes it "possible to disguise under one's own traits a phantasy person endowed with entirely fictitious greatness and torments" (14). These false affects, this false mourning, seem to have been the forms in which Johnson's literary experience expressed itself. He was close to suspecting that literature had imposed on him a spurious interiority, close enough to recognize such a phenomenon in theory, while regarding literary pathos and his particular vulnerability to it with ambivalence and distrust.

This distrust and its cause help to explain why, in his last work, Johnson pursued the task of making hopeless reparations to dead poets—why, that is, he sought the Oedipalization of literary space. The most exemplary of his hopeless reparations was in fact made in honor of his father. During a visit to Lichfield in 1781, Johnson disappeared for some hours; it transpired that he had been standing, hat in hand, at the corner in Uttoxeter where his father had used to set up his bookstall. In the fall before the winter in which he died, Michael Johnson had asked his son to make the trip to Uttoxeter market for him, but Johnson refused. He was now running this errand, fifty years late (Boswell 1357; Bate, *Samuel Johnson* 129). This private ceremony has usually been interpreted as a simple kind of penance. Yet it seems strange that Johnson allowed himself so literal-minded and eccentric a ritual. I am inclined to think of it as more wishful than penitential, as a resumption rather than an exorcism. Johnson was busy remembering himself as a son. As in *The Lives of the Poets,* he wished to return to the Oedipal organization of the world, in response to the dubiety of literary experience, out of nostalgia for human authority.

CHAPTER 3

The Grimness of the Truth

> Mais depuis que Swann était si triste, ressentant toujours cette espèce de frisson qui précède le moment où l'on va pleurer, il avait le même besoin de parler du chagrin qu'un assassin a de parler de son crime. En entendent la princesse lui dire que la vie était une chose affreuse, il éprova la même douceur que si elle avait lui parlé d'Odette.
>
> Proust, *Un Amour de Swann*

When little Jane Eyre first meets her school friend, the doomed melancholiac Helen Burns, this saintly child is sitting out in the cold, reading *Rasselas*. Unlike the children whom Johnson resigns to the world of fairy tales, Helen Burns has precociously learned to appreciate his cheerless novel. "I like it," she says in sober approval. Hazlitt, who found that reading Johnson gave him the willies, did not like it at all. To judge by his language, Johnson's writing seriously shocked Hazlitt, shocked him, as Johnson himself had been shocked by *King Lear*, in its open effort to be frightening, alienating, and horrible. In terms that recall the formidable conventions of Greek theater, he characterized Johnson's prose as violently denaturalizing: "We can no more distinguish the most familiar objects in his descriptions of them, than we can a well-known face under a huge painted mask" (102). And he was appalled by *Rasselas*, which he took for "the most melancholy and debilitating moral speculation that ever was put forth" (102). This strain of "melancholy," darkness, or severity does tend to dominate Johnson's work, and in forms surprisingly manifold, which I will be exploring below. Whatever relation it bears to his emotional melancholia, at any rate the darkness of his writing turns out, oddly enough, to corroborate his painful associations with literature and that vague dread of it we examined in the last chapter. The very painful and formidable qualities of literature that impressed and disturbed Johnson became just what he sought to recover, cultivate, refine, and strengthen in his own style. Johnson invented and perfected this prose style out of regard for some imperative to see, speak, convey, and believe in the grimness of the truth. In this way, he invented for English prose the syntax and the cadence of fatality. How, where, and why did he learn to do this, or to wish to do this? Whence did this imperative spring?

The Love of Mimesis

Boswell long ago found it curious that, though he was so moved by "pathetic" poetry as to cry over it in public, Johnson never wrote anything of a "pathetic character" himself. Indeed, he did not write in the deliberately sentimental mode that was popular during Boswell's lifetime. Yet Johnson was a serious, even obsessive reader, the most powerful and influential of his times, and his reading clearly shaped the aims and forms of his writing. His relentless severity answered to something in his experience of literature—though what it was remains to be seen.

To elucidate this question, let me begin with a passage that illuminates the first principle of Johnson's reading, what I will call his "love of mimesis," his belief—sometimes acknowledged and sometimes not—that literature tells the deep truth. This passage does not belong to any of his critical remarks about mimesis itself, whose technical meaning is not relevant to this discussion but belongs rather to the body of his quotations and paraphrases of literature. When, in *Rambler* no. 121, Johnson wishes to make manifest the commanding power of invention that compelled Homer's followers weakly to imitate him, he distinguishes his paraphrase of the *Odyssey* by a spare, grave style. After arguing that Virgil borrowed from Homer with a confused eagerness destructive to his own poem, Johnson suddenly begins to describe the scene of Odysseus in Hades—with the suddenness of passionate solemnity, that is: "When Ulysses visited the infernal regions, he found among the heroes that perished at Troy, his competitor Ajax, who, when the arms of Achilles were adjudged to

Ulysses, died by his own hand in the madness of disappointment. He still appeared to resent, as on earth, his loss and disgrace. Ulysses endeavoured to pacify him with praises and submission; but Ajax walked away without reply" (4:283).

Resuming his commentary, Johnson sets off this sad and stately paraphrase by launching into a vigorous sample of his own ornate periodic style. Effusion follows the syncope of Ajax's silence in this miniature "Knocking at the Gate." In appreciation, Johnson writes, "This passage has always been considered as eminently beautiful; because Ajax, the haughty chief, the unlettered soldier, of unshaken courage, of immoveable constancy, but without the power of recommending his assertions by any other argument than the sword, had no way of making his anger known but by gloomy sullenness, and dumb ferocity" (4:283). But when he returns to the comparison with Virgil and takes up the parallel incident in the *Aeneid,* Johnson adopts a clipped, journalistic hypotaxis that strips the *Aeneid* of all the authority with which his dark cadence had mantled Homer: "When Aeneas is sent by Virgil to the shades, he meets Dido the queen of Carthage, whom his perfidy has hurried to the grave; he accosts her with tenderness and excuses; but the lady turns away like Ajax in mute disdain. She turns away like Ajax, but she resembles him in none of those qualities which give either dignity or propriety to silence" (4:284). Besides its patriarchal purposes, Johnson's use of the words "dignity" and "propriety," which he often musters in the context of evaluative criticism, sheds strange light on the question of the authority that he accords to poems. It is, after all, his own prose style that has invested Ajax, and Homer in general, with dignity and propriety. These are terms that he imports from a classist vocabulary to justify or illuminate or anthropomorphize the floating authority of truthfulness with which a work has impressed him. They are names for tragic affect in particular: Homer is convincingly grim, where Virgil is only spuriously so. How remarkable that this form of authority—the sound of truth—has to be colored with sadness and darkness.

My analysis of these subtle changes in style is meant to suggest not that Johnson thought them through but, on the contrary, that they were automatic reproductions of instinctive responses to his reading, or "imitations without authority." It is as automatic responses that they reflect the archaic "love of mimesis." The love of mimesis is a tautological phenomenon in which the truth held to be mimetically reproduced by literature actually begins in literature and will be apprehended everywhere as a kind of truth wandering at large. A passage from Johnson's "Life of Otway" will show Johnson's enchantment with this floating truth. I choose this passage because it concerns the truth not of literature but of empirical fact and thus exemplifies how it is that, even (or especially) in as committed a realist as Johnson, empirical truth cannot help wearing the colors of the other truth—the literary authority of truthfulness.

Near the end of the "Life of Otway," after having described Otway's works, Johnson concludes suddenly, "All this was performed before he was thirty-four years old; for he died April 14, 1685, in a manner which I am unwilling to mention" (*Lives* 1:173). Johnson's idiosyncratic lexicon of "willing" and "hoping" deserves some examination, since it determines the tone of this passage. The protestation of reluctance here is serious in form because Johnson uses the words "willing" and "unwilling" for defensive reactions of deep emotional necessity. An *Idler* proclaims that "man is seldom willing to let fall the opinion of his own dignity" (no. 88, 274). And Johnson himself wrote to Hill Boothby, a dear friend whose death put an end to his thoughts of remarriage, "I love you and honour you, and am very unwilling to lose you" (*Letters* 1:121). The "will" expresses need and desire that is wild, founded on illusion or defiance of life, and thus susceptible if not doomed to disappointment. Like willingness, Johnson's hope often means blindness to the truth. But sometimes, especially as used in the first person, "hope" can signify an orientation toward the truth that is not defensively apotropaic but sighted, fragile, and apprehensive. As Johnson wrote Lucy Porter, "To be sick, and to see nothing but sickness and death is but a gloomy state, but I hope better times even in this world will come" (*Letters* 4:22).

After his weighty, ominous pause, Johnson's paragraph on Otway expands into the retelling of the poet's woeful death—several retellings, in fact, increasingly detailed and magnified, like the enhancements of a photograph.

> All this was performed before he was thirty-four years old; for he died April 14, 1685, in a manner which I am unwilling to mention.

Having been compelled by his necessities to contract debts, and hunted, as is supposed, by the terriers of the law, he retired to a publick house on Tower-hill, where he is said to have died of want; or, as it is related by one of his biographers, by swallowing, after a long fast, a piece of bread which charity had supplied. He went out, as is reported, almost naked, in the rage of hunger, and finding a gentleman in a neighboring coffee-house, asked him for a shilling. The gentleman gave him a guinea; and Otway going away bought a roll, and was choaked with the first mouthful. (*Lives* 1:173)

Johnson now retreats from this horrible story and from the dramatic prose that seems so involved with it, despite the tension-creating disclaimers ("as is supposed," "as it is related," "as is reported"). His qualification is, as it turns out, no less charismatically severe than his narrative: "All this, I hope, is not true; and there is this ground of better hope, that Pope, who lived near enough to be well informed, relates in Spence's memorials, that he died of a fever caught by violent pursuit of a thief that had robbed one of his friends" (173).

The language of Johnson's disavowal is dubious, however, since this happier version of events belongs to the world of tenuous wishes that Johnson's hope always gestures toward. Even if its empirical accuracy is in question, the bitterer story somehow lies closer to the truth, as Johnson's final judgment intimates: "But that indigence, and its concomitants, sorrow and despondency, pressed hard upon him, has never been denied, whatever immediate cause might bring him to the grave" (173). Truthfulness—the grim sound of truth—has its own power of persuasion, and though its floating authority is not that of empirical truth, it cannot but be felt as if it were. Johnson's "unwillingness" to tell the cruel but not necessarily accurate story ensures that it will sound deep and true.

The form of truth developed under the love of mimesis has the status of the preterite. That is to say, the truth to which literary pathos bears witness is a dark truth and therefore perpetually troubling, exiled, and ignored. This was Weil's programmatic definition of truth, as we have seen, and it was because she held this definition that she took literature to speak for the outcast and the pariah, for human beings who have been "passed over" in preterition. According to Johnson, too, the truth is deliberately neglected because it reproaches actuality: "Truth is, indeed, not often welcome for its own sake; it is generally unpleasing because contrary to our wishes and opposite to our practice; and as our attention naturally follows our interests, we hear unwillingly what we are afraid to know, and soon forget what we have no inclination to impress upon our memories" (*Rambler* no. 96, 4:149). The exile of the truth is confirmed even by Johnson's supposedly complacent rationalism, since he usually invokes "reason" exactly where it is missing: "Nothing surely can be more unworthy of a reasonable nature, than to continue in a state so opposite to real happiness, as that all the peace of solitude, and felicity of meditation, must arise from resolutions of forsaking it" (*Rambler* no. 155, 5:63). "Surely nothing can be more unreasonable than to lose the will to please, when we are conscious of the power, or show more cruelty than to chuse any kind of influence before that of kindness" (*Rambler* no. 72, 4:16). The truth of reason ineffectually protests against the ways of a world to which neither kindness nor reason belongs. The will of life protests against the darkness of the truth that is its enemy. It *is* a dark enemy, despite the familiar metaphor of illumination: "The torch of truth shows much that we cannot, and all that we would not see" (*Rambler* no. 10, 3:58). In this sharp paradox, Truth brings the shadowy truth to light. Under the contradictory conception of truth fostered by the authority of literature, truth is at once the grim truth of actuality—which everyone can see—and the deep truth of grim reality—which everyone avoids seeing. No matter what, here, as in the story of Otway's death, the truth declines toward darkness, as if to corroborate Weil's fierce affirmation: "Truth is on the side of death."

What does it mean to believe in literature as in the truth? This passage from the "Life of Cowley" may be said to reflect the accrediting or "naturalization" of literature by regretting an instance of its failure:

> Cowley's *Mistress* has no power of seduction: "she plays round the head, but comes not at the heart." Her beauty and absence, her kindness and cruelty, her disdain and inconstancy, produce no correspondence of emotion. His poetical account of the virtues of plants, and colours of flowers, is not perused with more sluggish frigidity. The compositions are such as might have been written for penance by a

hermit, or for hire by a philosophical rhymer who had only heard of another sex; for they turn the mind only on the writer, whom, without thinking on a woman but as the subject for his task, we sometimes esteem as learned, and sometimes despise as trifling, always admire as ingenious, and always condemn as unnatural. (*Lives* 1:34–35)

Johnson finds Cowley's poem "unnatural" and unpleasing because it does not succeed in imposing on us with the force of reality. Yet in his implicit demand for mimesis Johnson is asking for a strangely suspended and uncertain variety of truth. Here he complains that we do not believe in Cowley's love of the "Mistress" or even in her existence. But earlier he had informed us that there really was no mistress and that "the reader's esteem for the work and the author" was bound to suffer from this knowledge. He went on to suggest (and oddly enough, as was shown in the last chapter) that Cowley became himself enraptured and enthralled by this "shadow," this "airy nothing." Johnson now argues something like the opposite—that Cowley is pedantically solipsistic, and the mistress is patently unreal. Questions of her historical reality are no longer the issue; her shadowiness in the poem itself dissuades us. Thus the poem's facticiousness is now found to be of an aesthetic order and no longer of an empirical one. Alongside the demand for mimetic illusion—alongside the love of mimesis—the criteria of empirical truth fail. It is ruinous, not that Cowley's love should be a lie, but that it should sound like a lie.

To require persuasive mimetic illusion in itself hardly seems unreasonable or surprising. But it deserves reflection that criteria of an aesthetic order should demand to be expressed as empirical criteria. Johnson explains his dissatisfaction by faulting the nonexistent mistress, whom he finds to be, as it were, insufficiently attractive and interesting: "Cowley's mistress has no power of seduction.... Her beauty and absence, her kindness and cruelty, her disdain and inconstancy, produce no correspondence of emotion." But, on the other hand, the failings may be those of Cowley himself, whose poem reveals him to have been a narrow virtuoso and a solipsist: "The compositions are such as might have been written for penance by a hermit, or for hire by a philosophical rhymer who had only heard of another sex; for they turn the mind only on the writer," and so on. By anthropomorphizing certain aspects of the poem, Johnson casts its deficiencies as personal, human deficiencies of the mistress or of the poet. What he finally draws out of the poem is the character of the writer, a "learned" and "ingenious" but "trifling" and "unnatural" man.

It is not that this anthropomorphism ever becomes so vivid as to obscure its status as a figure of speech. In fact, it is unsettled by other, depersonifying moments such as the allusion to Cowley's "poetical account of the virtues of plants, and colours of flowers," or the application to the mistress of the miniaturizing and almost grotesque line "she plays round the head, but comes not at the heart." Yet Johnson's anthropomorphism serves to sustain the metaphor of his deepest criticism—that the poem "produces no correspondence of emotion," that it does not "come at the heart" because it does not concern real and lovable people. Johnson resorts to anthropomorphism because this aesthetic problem insists on being formulated as an empirical one, as a problem of unreality and untruth. The "unreal" is then placed in a close relationship with the "unnatural," bordering on identity with it. As the final word of this condemnation, the word "unnatural" itself hovers between a literary meaning, "artificial," and a psychological one, "perverse."

In evaluating literary works, Johnson uses the concept of nature tautologically. When a poem is unlikable, it is unnatural because it is unlikable. In all of Johnson's pronouncements on the naturalness of a given work, there lurks the possibility of an easy reversal between the criteria of the natural and the criteria of literary excellence. About metaphysical wit, for example, he writes, "That confusion of images may entertain for a moment; but being unnatural, it soon grows wearisome" (*Lives* 1:34). One might rather say that metaphysical wit seems unnatural whenever it is, for whatever reason, wearisome. Later Johnson addresses himself to the charge that, instead of being "general" and natural, Cowley is pedantic: "If by pedantry is meant that minute knowledge which is derived from particular sciences and studies, in opposition to the general notions supplied by a wide survey of life and nature, Cowley certainly errs, by introducing pedantry far more frequently than Tasso" (*Lives* 1:46). Again one might think that it is the "general notions" of literature that provide the sweep and feeling of "wide survey" and that it is this trope of sight that governs "the wide survey of life and nature." If

Johnson's definitions of the natural can be thus turned about, what facilitates this reversal? The terms "nature," "natural," and the like are being employed to characterize a nebulous literary power with which they have nothing to do. But the choice of terms is not arbitrary, since the love of mimesis demands that what in literature should most seem to be is true to us, faithful to us and our experience, though in fact it is our fidelity to literature that this demand, or wish, reflects.

The "Life of Cowley" constitutes the manifesto of Johnson's aesthetic priorities. Here, in his assessment of metaphysical poetry, he formulates those demands of the love of mimesis that he elsewhere leaves inexplicit or temporarily suspends in favor of a formalist agenda (an agenda that, though not illusory and not trivial, is finally supervenient). Indeed, it is his first complaint about the metaphysical poets that "they cannot be said to have imitated anything" (*Lives* 1:14). This fundamental mistake condemned them to be learned and clever without being persuasive, moving, or profound. Johnson translates their aesthetic failings into a grave moral incapacity on the part of the poets, whom he likes to describe as uncaring, perverse, ambitious, and blind. Here, as in his anthropomorphism of "The Mistress," it is the occulted love of mimesis that leads, among other things, to the conflation of a rhetoric with an ethic.

Laying out the criteria by which the metaphysical poets are to be found wanting, Johnson begins, "If . . . that be considered as Wit, which is at once natural and new, that which, though not obvious, is, upon its first production, acknowledged to be just; if it be that, which he that never found it, wonders how he missed; to wit of this kind the metaphysical poets have seldom risen. Their thoughts are often new, but seldom natural; they are not obvious, but neither are they just; and the reader, far from wondering that he missed them, wonders more frequently by what perverseness of industry they were ever found" (*Lives* 1:14). Johnson calls this definition of wit more "noble" and "adequate" than Pope's ("ne'er so well expressed") because it concentrates on intellectual instead of rhetorical innovations. But the complex of terms involved here is even more suggestive. As the criterion of the highest literary value, Johnson proposes the marriage of nature, novelty, and justice. But what is at first called justice ("upon its first production, acknowledged to be just") turns out to a form of ideal coincidence ("which he that never found it, wonders how he missed"). This form of coincidence is like that which Johnson sought to find between the world and literature. But here, coincidence is eerily isolated; it is not that a good work coincides with anything but that it simply produces a groundless feeling of coincidence. With the confusion of terms in this passage, the "just," or true, the "natural," and the "new" are drawn into the orbit of groundless coincidence, and it seems at last that, no less than surprise and novelty, truth and nature are chimeras that belong to literary experience.

Because the "truth" exemplified in literature already has a literary character, some interesting inconsistencies arise when Johnson puts literature to the test of truth. These inconsistencies, some of which he pointed out himself, have to do with the contradiction between a poem's explicit claims and its affect. Empirical truth cannot in fact compete with the affect of truth; so it is suggested when Johnson candidly remarks about a line in Cowley, "It is the odd fate of this thought to be worse for being true" (*Lives* 1:31). Cowley had written an elegy for his friend Lord Hervey, which, like "Lycidas," Johnson found to contain too little mourning and too much virtuosity: "But when he wishes to make us to weep, he forgets to weep himself, and diverts his sorrow by imagining how his crown of bays, if he had it, would *crackle* in the *fire*. It is the odd fate of this thought to be the worse for being true. The bay-leaf crackles remarkably as it burns; as therefore this property was not assigned it by chance, the mind must be thought sufficiently at ease that could attend to such minuteness of physiology" (*Lives* 1:30–31). The truths of empirical science—that is, "natural" truths—absolutely detract from the poem's real truth, the truth of mourning. Something other than truth is required to convince us of the truth here.

In other judgments as well, Johnson's accuracy to the reader's response threatens the coherence of the theory of mimesis. When he criticizes Milton's allegory of Sin and Death, he explains, in terms that seem both convincing and illogical, "To give [allegorical figures] any real employment, or ascribe to them any material agency, is to make them allegorical no longer, but to shock the mind by ascribing effects to nonentity" (*Lives* 1:133). This analysis begs the question of nonentity in the case of other fictional characters. Johnson's repugnance to the allegory in Milton reflects the contradictory consequences of the love of mimesis, which renders fictions of human character real and true, while, in contrast to them, it makes ambiguously subjectivized characters seem "shocking."[1]

The reader recoils from the violation of an illusion that, on the one hand, she or he in no way requires to be metaphysically consistent. Thus the theory of mimesis fails to accommodate the responses instinctive to the love of mimesis. The theory of mimesis is generated by the love of mimesis. That is to say, the theory that "literature reflects the world and its truth" evolves unawares from an earlier, more primitive response: "I love literature so much that to me it sounds like the truth of the world." But because the love of mimesis is original and instinctive and has nothing to do with "nature," reflection, or empirical truth, it is perpetually distressing and entangling its own theory, its own rationale. And yet, though the love of mimesis is genuinely groundless, it is not a mystification, because there is no more authoritative truth about life by whose light it might be revealed as error. It is an illusion so radical that it cannot be subjected to the paradigm of error and truth.[2]

What is the future of this super illusion, the archaic and stubborn love of mimesis? Johnson always insisted on a particular chronology of reading in which the pleasures of fiction slowly wane on mature minds that have learned to distinguish and revere the truth. The simple, and dangerous, joy of representation is reserved for children, naive readers who smile at Milton's war in heaven and disregard its metaphysical confusion: "The confusion of spirit and matter which pervades the whole narration of the war of heaven fills it with incongruity; and the book, in which it is related, is, I believe, the favourite of children, and gradually neglected as knowledge is increased" (*Lives* 1:133). Johnson turns childhood into a figure for naive reading, as we saw in the "Preface to Shakespeare," where he explains that incredible fables could thrive until the Renaissance because "nations, like individuals, have their infancy." But the infant is destined to grow up. According to a *Rambler*, literature that once seemed engaging and delightful gradually comes to be rejected, though not without labor and difficulty:

> While the judgement is yet uninformed and unable to compare the draughts of fiction with their originals, we are delighted with

improbable adventures, impracticable virtues and inimitable characters: But, in proportion as we have more opportunities of acquainting ourselves with living nature, we are sooner disgusted with copies in which there appears no resemblance. We first discard absurdity and impossibility, then exact greater and greater degrees of probability, but at last become cold and insensible to the charms of falsehood, however specious, and, from the imitations of truth, which are never perfect, transfer our affections to truth itself" (no. 151, 5:39).

Though Johnson treats truth as utterly real and distinct, his account of how it emerges has the effect of making it seem tenuous—as a latecomer to whom we have only transferred our indulgence and whose integrity is blurred by closely jostling "imitations." Affection for the truth is anaclitically derived from affection for literature; in other words, the love of mimesis produces solicitude for the truth. But this outcome leads in turn to disappointment, since it will be devotion to mimesis, to literature, that will make a reader impatient with the imperfect "imitations of truth" that are to be found there. Such is the source of Johnson's impatience with pastoral and with "Lycidas" in particular, whose artificial and implausible mourning provoked his condemnation: "It is not to be considered as the effusion of real passion; for passion runs not after remote allusions and obscure opinions.... In this poem, there is no nature, for there is no truth" (*Lives* 1:115).

The love of mimesis stimulates both a passionate solicitude for truth, arising from the conviction of its substantiality, and an attitude of nonchalance about the truth-value of specific propositions. Thus Johnson could gaily "talk for victory" although he was restless and severe, to the point of torment, about the imperative to truth. He "talked for victory" when, for example, he summarily pronounced, "No man but a blockhead ever wrote, except for money." This aphorism has never been credited with sincerity, not even by Boswell, who first quoted it under the name of "that strange opinion, which his indolent disposition made him utter" (731). His "indolence" was of a Proustian or Blanchotian order: Johnson was too unwilling, not too lazy, to write, except when he had a financial or humanitarian incentive—that is, a disguise for writing, under which it could appear as a friend of "the living world." When Johnson said that not only he but "no man ever wrote, except for money," he expressed a wish: the wish that writing could be a useful, affectless occupation, a task worthy of modest and responsible citizens, instead of being wild, sad, narcissistic, and autoteleological. Everything in Johnson's miserable life as an author certifies that he experienced writing's refusal to let the writer take part in the world, in goodness, and in work. It is because of this refusal, and not because of the otherworldliness of literary genius (as Boswell imagined), that there can be no "writing for money." Thus Johnson surely meant to torture himself by admiring, repeating, and even engraving on his watch the Bible's strict injunction "Work, for the night cometh, in which no man can work."

This symbiosis of Johnson's writing and Johnson's masochism has always been recognized. Yet the denial of writing does not provide the only motive for the deep words of his diverting claim that "no man . . . ever wrote, except for money." This stark phrase "no man" seems to echo from august pronouncements, among them the Bible's "no man can work," and Shakespeare's "nor no man ever loved." But the context and meaning of these echoes have little relevance. It is really the sound of austerity, or the memory of an austerity of thought, that Johnson is irresistibly imitating. To repeat the phrase "no man ever," with its grandeur and austerity, is, in some dark and unsettled way, to meet the standards imposed by the search for truth. And here these standards are clearly intertwined with the standards of literary power. Literature provides criteria of truth—and for this reason, literature and the sense of truth each appears to have the other for its end. But because of the nature of literary pathos, when literature provides the criteria of truth, then the truth will be, as Weil would have it, on the side of death. Thus it was his fidelity to literature that Johnson expressed in the form of his gloom and severity.

The Severe Style

When Hazlitt described *Rasselas* as "the most melancholy and debilitating speculation that was ever put forth," he was responding seriously to something that is really there in Johnson's novel. *Rasselas is* discouraging in so far as, though the moral of the work appears early on, it is never, as indeed it never can be, recognized, instituted, or transcended: when a group of learned men hears the story of the hermit who vacillates unhappily between society and solitude, one, "who appeared more affected with the narrative than the rest," sadly prophesies that the hermit will continue his fruitless changes until he dies, "for the hope of happiness . . . is so strongly impressed, that the longest experience is not able to efface it" (85). One of the *Rambler*'s wickedly bathetic metaphors brings alive the vanity of this restless hope and the inevitability of its power to obscure the truth: "Whoever feels great pain naturally hopes for ease from change of posture; he changes it, and finds himself equally tormented: and of the same kind are the expedients by which we endeavor to obviate or elude those uneasinesses, to which mortality will always be subject" (no. 45, 3:245).

Rasselas purports to be a propaideutic journey, a journey to find out the means of happiness—that is, to find out that there are no such means; but how are the prince and princess to learn this impossible truth, which not even the "longest experience" can persuade us to accept or believe? Naturally, the prince and princess exhibit ample resistance to the appalling "lessons" that their teacher, Imlac, and their text, the miseries of the world, have to show them. When the prince has grown discontented with the "Happy Valley" and determined to exchange its tedium for the excitements of the wide world, he hears from Imlac that human life is hardly endurable under any conditions. But, the prince insists, "I am not yet willing . . . to suppose that happiness is so parsimoniously distributed to mortals" (51). Having escaped, and finding himself melancholy in Cairo, where all the inhabitants seem content, the prince complains to Imlac, who informs him that every one is miserable at heart, but "we are long before we are convinced that happiness is never to be found, and each believes it possessed by others, to keep alive the hope of obtaining it for himself" (66). The prince has unlearned this lesson by the end of the conversation, at which point he declares, "I have here the world before me, I will review it at leisure: surely happiness is somewhere to be found" (68).[3]

Having agreed to divide the work of investigating the conditions of the world, the prince and princess then refuse to believe each other's unhappy

The Grimness of the Truth

discoveries. The princess concludes that age defeats the tenderness between parents and their children; but at this the prince balks: "Surely... you must have been unfortunate in your choice of acquaintance: I am unwilling to believe, that the most tender of all relations is thus impeded in its effects by natural necessity" (97). She assures him that it is, and that marriage itself is no less afflicted; when he then declares against marriage, she reminds him sharply that the alternative has nothing at all to recommend it. Cornered and exasperated, he turns his severity against her, mobilizing the insight he has gained into the poverty of philosophy: "The prince, having considered his sister's observations, told her, that she had surveyed life with prejudice, and supposed misery where she did not find it. 'Your narrative,' says he, 'throws yet a darker gloom upon the prospects of futurity: the predictions of Imlac were but faint sketches of the evils painted by Nekayah'" (99). Indeed, these abstract "narratives," these demographical surveys of misery, are so flatly dismal, so oppressive and riveting in a temporary, spurious way (like *Rasselas*), that Imlac dissipates a kind of a spell when he reenters, saying, "It seems to me . . . that while you are making the choice of life, you neglect to live" (111).

At the end of the novel there is a final crescendo of resistance in response to the appearance of the most "debilitating" character, the sane, good man who has reached a ripe old age. In his clear-sighted gloom, he represents an antithesis to the grand, mad Astronomer. His testimony is resolutely astringent without being seductive or exciting. Because of his age and long grief, "nothing is now of much importance" to him.

> Youth is delighted with applause, because it is considered as the earnest of some future good, and because the prospect of life is far extended: but to me, who am now declining to decrepitude, there is little to be feared from the malevolence of men, and yet less to be hoped from their affection or esteem. Something they may yet take away, but they can give me nothing. Riches would now be useless, and high employment would be pain. My retrospect of life recalls to my view many opportunities of good neglected, much time squandered upon trifles, and more lost in idleness and vacancy. I leave many great designs unattempted, and many great attempts unfinished. My

mind is burthened with no heavy crime, and therefore I compose myself to tranquillity; endeavor to abstract my thoughts from hopes and cares, which, though reason knows them to be vain, still try to keep their old possession of the heart; expect, with serene humility, that hour which nature cannot long delay; and hope to possess in a better state that happiness which here I could not find, and that virtue which here I have not attained. (156)

There is really nothing to say to these definitively unfriendly remarks, and so, Johnson adds with pleasant understatement, "he rose and went away, leaving his audience not much elated with the hope of long life." Against so unsentimental and unassailable an authority, the young people can produce only specious counterarguments:

The prince consoled himself with remarking, that it was not reasonable to be disappointed by this account; for age had never been considered as the season of felicity, and, if it was possible to be easy in decline and weakness, it was likely that the days of vigour and alacrity might be happy: that the noon of life might be bright, if the evening could be calm.

The princess suspected that age was querulous and malignant, and delighted to repress the expectations of those who had newly entered the world. She had seen the possessors of estates look with envy on their heirs, and known many who enjoy pleasure no longer than they can confine it to themselves.

Pekuah conjectured, that the man was older than he appeared, and was willing to impute his complaints to delirious dejection; or else supposed that he had been unfortunate, and was therefore discontented: "For nothing, said she, is more common than to call our own condition, the condition of life." (157)

At this point their contentiousness is thematized as denial, and the inevitability of resistance to the novel's "lessons," the inevitability of resistance to the truth of unhappiness, is acknowledged in Imlac's response: he "smiled at the comforts which they could so readily procure to themselves, and remembered, that at the same age, he was equally confident of unmingled prosperity, and equally fertile of consolatory expedients." In the last chapter, the three young people, along with Imlac and the astronomer, entertain themselves by divulging their hopes for the future, but for once "of these wishes they had formed they well knew that none could be obtained." That their knowledge should take this comically self-defeating form points up the paradoxical conclusion of *Rasselas*. To "pursue the phantoms of hope" is to live in perilous and contemptible delusion, while abjuring the hopes that tie one to life means descending into the old man's posthumous twilight. As Johnson put it in *Idler* no. 58, "It is necessary to hope, tho' hope should be always deluded, for hope itself is happiness, and its frustrations, however frequent, are yet less dreadful than its extinction." The comfort of hope "keeps life in motion" by effacing its hopelessness.

In fact, the hope to which Rasselas and his sister cling is only one of the names for life's willful obliviousness to itself, an obliviousness that is always diverting us from the truth, especially truth of the most fundamental kind: this obliviousness ensures first and foremost the impossibility of our comprehending the nature and the certainty of death. Johnson returns again and again to the volatility of the thought of death, which, "however forcible at every new impression, is every moment fading from the mind" (*Idler* no. 103, 315). That "life is short" is, he says, "a well-known and well-attested position . . . which may be heard among mankind by an attentive auditor, many times a day, but which never yet within my reach left any impression upon the mind" (*Rambler* no. 71, 4:8). This contrasts with the hope of happiness, "so strongly impressed, that the longest experience is not able to efface it." Death is so eluctable, so forgettable, that "some eastern monarch . . . kept an officer in his house, whose employment it was to remind him of his mortality, by calling out every morning at a stated hour, 'Remember, prince, that thou shalt die'" (*Rambler* no. 17, 3:92). This crucial form of obliviousness—the ignorance of death—is a subset of that more willful resistance to truth that condemns the living to blindness and repetition, to the treadmill. With his most fascinating relentlessness, Johnson studied this syndrome in his friend Richard Savage, a walker of pitifully narrow rounds, about whom Johnson concludes early enough in the "Life of Savage" for it to be bitterly anticlimatic,

By imputing none of his miseries to himself, he continued to act upon the same principles, and to follow the same path; was never made wiser by his sufferings, nor preserved by one misfortune from falling into another. He proceeded throughout his life to tread the same steps on the same circle; always applauding his past conduct, or at least forgetting it, to amuse himself with phantoms of happiness, which were dancing before him; and willingly turned his eyes from the light of reason, when it would have discovered the illusion, and shewn him, what he never wished to see, his real state. (*Lives* 2:143)

Beneath this human blankness (the blind tenacity of wishes, the monotonous failure of learning), another trend is working all the time, leading the stupid subject to an end in disappointment and suffering. *Rasselas* and other of Johnson's works seek to moralize this shadowy, impersonal force. Like Weil, Johnson means to align his works, in content and style, with the severity and harshness of fate—to be true to it, capture it, match it, appease it. To the extent that the force cannot be mastered by learning, Johnson's works, in their alliance with it, cannot serve a didactic purpose—though the fierce impersonality of their sentiments answers to the ferocity of their subject. The novel's "propaideutic" appearances are therefore something of a ruse, a solemn joke of the sort that Hazlitt could justly have called "debilitating."

The paradox that *Rasselas* teaches cannot be learned except as a kind of dreary sentiment left to float on the mind's surface. The peculiar unassimilability of its "lesson" follows from the staged character of its project—to make an intellectual inquiry into suffering, to take a "survey" of all the forms, the properties and percentages of unhappiness. This technique—reconnoitering life's misery from the skies—is a favorite of Johnson's. Sublimely comprehensive and perfectly bleak, it will be remembered from "The Vanity of Human Wishes," especially its opening lines: "Let observation with extensive view, / Survey mankind, from China to Peru; / Remark each anxious toil, each eager strife, / And watch the busy scenes of crouded life" (1–4).

Johnson was not above acknowledging that this project can seem comical and perverse, as he has a correspondent to the *Rambler* suggest:

> Sir—Though you seem to have taken a view sufficiently extensive of the miseries of life, and have employed much of your speculation on mournful subjects, you have not yet exhausted the whole stock of human infelicity. There is still a species of wretchedness which escapes your observation, though it might supply you with many sage remarks and salutary cautions. . . . I cannot but imagine the start of attention awakened by this welcome hint; and at this instant see the Rambler snuffing his candle, rubbing his spectacles, stirring his fire, locking out interruption, and settling himself in his easy chair, that he may enjoy a new calamity without disturbance. (no. 109, 4:215)

This is an irresistibly witty and candid admission of the voracity of gloom—that philosopher's gloom which which for some odd reason demands to be fed. Hester Thrale, whose account of Johnson is less idealized than the accounts of most of his other contemporary biographers, tells a more serious story about how determined, if not cruel, his pessimism could be.

> Mr Johnson did not like any one who said they were happy, or who said any one else was so. "It is all *cant* (he would cry), the dog knows he is miserable all the time." A friend whom he loved exceedingly, told him on some occasion notwithstanding, that his wife's sister was really happy, and called upon the lady to confirm his assertion, which she did somewhat roundly as we say, and with an accent and manner capable of offending Mr. Johnson, if her position had not been sufficient, without any thing more, to put him in very ill humour. "If your sister-in-law is really the contented being she professes herself Sir (said he), her life gives the lie to every research of humanity; for she is happy without health, without beauty, without money, without understanding." This story he told me himself; and when I expressed something of the horror I felt, "The same stupidity (said he) which prompted her to extol felicity she never felt, hindered her from feeling what shocks you on repetition. I tell you, the woman is ugly, and sickly, and foolish, and poor; and would it not make a man hang himself, to hear such a creature say, it was happy?" (181–82)

It behooves us to take this anecdote not as a revelation of some particular perversity in Johnson—despite its typically horrid tinge of misogyny—but as an example of the uncompromising rigor that is practiced by fatalism. Or, to be more precise, it is an example of literary opportunism, of Johnson's indulging himself in a severity whose charm is intertwined with the allurements of incantatory formulas ("make a man hang himself") and poetic meters ("ugly, and sickly, and foolish, and poor").[4]

Johnson portrayed the omnipotence of fatality in which he so believed with the utmost energy in "The Vanity of Human Wishes" and most famously in its stinging aphorism "Fate wings with ev'ry wish th'afflictive dart." "Fate" can be a neutral word, meaning one's lot or portion, whatever it might be; but here it is assuming its darker cast, like the Greek word "moira," which means "share," then "destiny," and then "death." "Fate" is not neutral in "The Vanity of Human Wishes," because, the poem insists, it is not neutral in reality. Its choice is to turn pleasure, talent, hope, and life against themselves, to turn them into the work of pain, "th'afflictive dart" that is dipped in the poison of unconscious self-destruction. "Fate" slides down the scale toward its harshest connotations: now it is fatality, it is death:

> Fate wings with ev'ry wish th'afflictive dart,
> Each gift of nature, and each grace of art,
> With fatal heat impetuous courage glows,
> With fatal sweetness elocution flows,
> Impeachment stops the speaker's pow'rful breath,
> And restless fire precipitates on death.
>
> (15–20)

There is nothing more chilling in Johnson than this notion of fate as fatality, a frightening law of life by which everything tends toward darkness because even good things carry within them the seeds of their own destruction. We have already heard this law of fate called by the name "natural necessity" when in *Rasselas,* the princess concludes that the tenderness of parents and children is by its structure doomed to decay. By natural necessity, "sweetness" and "heat" are more "fatal" than "impeachment" and "death." The word "fatal" appears regularly in "The Vanity of Human Wishes," where it moves easily from this application—as a pointedly transferred epithet—to its more familiar use as the modifier of words signifying destiny and death. Charles Albert, "the Bold Bavarian," aspired and rose high, but "the baffled prince in honour's flatt'ring bloom / Of hasty greatness finds the fatal doom" (251–52). Bishop Laud paid dearly for all his intellectual labor and "glittering eminence": "Mark'd out by dangerous parts he meets the shock, / And fatal Learning leads him to the block" (171–72).

To speak the truth in Johnson means to have fully internalized the law of fate, to have incorporated fatality. The characters in *Rasselas* who have arrived at wisdom and truthfulness are able to speak in the first person as if speaking of another whose fate is clear and bleak. We have already seen an example of this wisdom in the sane man, who describes his hopeless and lonely old age with cold, remote, and pitiless precision. Similarly, it is offered up as proof of the Astronomer's returning sanity that he can perceive and articulate the painful waste of his life. Even the young Rasselas, who can hardly have achieved their clearsightedness, reaches the point of being able to describe his motives and his actions without the "solace" of "polished periods" and sentimentalizing narcissism and instead with the severity of an omniscient narrator. Early in the novel, he had formulated melancholy generalizations "uttering them with a plaintive voice, yet with a look that discovered him to feel some complacence in his own perspicacity, and to receive some solace of the miseries of life, from consciousness of the delicacy with which he felt, and the eloquence with which he bewailed them" (14). By the end, his discourse occasionally, if only trivially, rises to the fierce impersonality of what the novel defines as wisdom, as when he declares for the catacombs, "I know not . . . what pleasure the sight of the catacombs can afford; but, since nothing else is offered, I am resolved to view them, and shall place this with many other things which I have done, because I would do something" (167).

In obedience to the commanding rigor of this discourse, Johnson practiced the use of it upon himself, like the old man in *Rasselas*. This will be readily perceived from his diaries and annals, which contain such expertly impersonal self-recriminations as this: "I have now spent fifty years in resolving, having from the earliest time almost that I can remember been forming schemes of a better life. I have done nothing; the need of doing therefore is pressing, since the time of doing is short" (*Diaries* 81). He sometimes employs this voice in his letters, where, it is true, he is generally more gentle on both himself and his correspondent—but where he is still capable of writing, sternly, "I have now learned the inconveniences of a winter campaign. But I hope home will make me amends for all my foolish sufferings" (*Letters* 3:378).

Fatality could hardly have failed to catch up with Johnson himself. The longest, most dramatic, detailed, and powerful portrait in *Rasselas* is that of the mad Astronomer, whose case exemplifies the useless dangers and sufferings of "literary solitude." This subject naturally provides the climax of *Rasselas,* which, in the midst of all its demystifications, has steadily held out knowledge, curiosity, and "the love of learning" as sources of real and darling joy. This darling, fateful passion is also lamented at length in "The Vanity of Human Wishes," where the scholar takes his place among the ranks of deluded agonists:

> When first the college rolls receive his name,
> The young enthusiast quits his ease for fame;
> Through all his veins the fever of renown
> Burns from the strong contagion of the gown;
> O'er Bodley's dome his future labours spread,
> And Bacon's mansion trembles o'er his head.
> Are these thy views? proceed, illustrious youth,
> And virtue guard thee to the throne of Truth!
> Yet should thy soul indulge the gen'rous heat,
> Till captive Science yields her last retreat;
> Should Reason guide thee with her brightest ray,
> And pour on misty Doubt resistless day,
> Should no false Kindness lure to loose delight,
> Nor Praise relax, nor Difficulty fright;
> Should tempting Novelty thy cell refrain;
> And Sloth effuse her opiate fumes in vain;
> Should Beauty blunt on fops her fatal dart,
> Nor claim the triumph of a letter'd heart;
> Should no disease thy torpid veins invade,

> Nor Melancholy's phantoms haunt thy shade;
> Yet hope not life from grief or danger free,
> Nor think the doom of man revers'd for thee:
> Deign on the passing world to turn thine eyes,
> And pause awhile from letters, to be wise;
> There mark what ills the scholar's life assail,
> Toil, envy, want, the patron and the jail.
> See nations slowly wise, and meanly just,
> To buried merit raise the tardy bust.
> If dreams yet flatter, once again attend,
> Hear Lydiat's life, and Galileo's end.
>
> (135–64)

When Johnson read his poem aloud to the Thrale family, he choked at that paragraph and "burst into a passion of tears" (Bate, *Samuel Johnson*, 107). There is no doubt that he believed this picture to be true—believed in the writer excoriated by the shirt of Nessus, burning in the self-immolation of a doomed love—because to believe that life is fateful and that the truth is harrowing and dark is to dread lest fatality has cast, above all, its long shadow over you. Johnson sought to invest his literary stance with the impersonal severity of fate, whose dire autonomy he succeeded in making all the more vivid. He thereby instilled himself with a sense of his own vulnerability, which his knowledge of fate could never temper, and so, with a superstitious horror of fate's revenge.

In this voice of fate lie the innovation and the brilliance of Johnson's prose style. It is the voice of the impartial surveyor, whose judgments are so precise and sharp that it can, for example, say about Ambrose Phillips, "He has added nothing to English poetry" (*Lives* 1:393), or about an action of Edmund Waller's, "The motive was illiberal and dishonest, and shewed that more than sixty years had not been able to teach him morality" (*Lives* 1:196). With such icy judgments, the voice of Johnson's prose aligns itself with the impersonality and severity of fate.

Johnson's prose pursues this identification not only in content but in form. Indeed, he aspired after the incantatory power of grimness in his style, and this is what spurred it to the vigor and authority for which it is admired. Certain pronounced formal qualities ensure that the affect of a sentence will always fall to its gravest.⁵ For example: "It is not uncommon for those who at their first entrance into the world were distinguished for attainments or abilities, to disappoint the hopes which they had raised, and to end in neglect and obscurity that life which they began in celebrity and honor" (*Rambler* no. 127, 4:312). This sentence of Johnson's is typical not only for its grim sentiment but for the syntax of inexorability that wings its grimness. The chilling effect springs from the pivotal demonstrative "that" in "that life," of which there is only one in this sentence, as in reality: "to end in neglect and obscurity that life which they began in celebrity and honor."

An inexorable severity informs the syntax of much of Johnson's prose. His sentences are notable for their deliberated pace and devastating conclusions, for the long suspense that finally yields a more absolute catastrophe. They can, for instance, stimulate a kind of false hope by offering a series of alternatives that turn out all to be bad, so that, instead of being expansive, this list becomes more bleak the more conscientiously it pursues thoroughness and detail. When an old and trusted advisor of Rasselas is rebuffed, he recovers quickly, because, "in the decline of life shame and grief are of short duration; whether it be that we bear easily what we have born long, or that, finding ourselves in age less regarded, we less regard others; or, that we look with slight regard upon afflictions, to which we know that the hand of death is about to put to end" (17). This collapse of hope occurs more precipitously in the failure of antithesis, in sentences whose structure promises contrast but which finally offer only a grim identity. Such is the depressing fate of parallelism in his famous dicta "Marriage has many pains, but celibacy has no pleasures" (99) and "Human life is every where a state in which much is to be endured, and little to be enjoyed" (50).⁶

Johnson will typically invert the syntax of a sentence to make its conclusion more ineluctable and shocking: for example, "Mrs. Kennedy, Queeny's Baucis, ended last week a long life of disease and poverty" (*Letters* 3:169). Or he will use what are called "delaying phrases" so that the crucial words, the sad truth, can be suspended until the last moment. The use of the impersonal subject "it" in phrases such as "it is" and "it must be confessed" serves this purpose. "It is one of the innumerable absurdities of pride, that we are never more impatient of direction, than in that part of life when we need it most" (*Rambler* no. 111, 4:230). "It is scarcely credible to what degree discernment may be dazzled by the mist of pride, and wisdom infatuated by the intoxication of flattery; or how low the genius may descend by successive gradations of servility, and how swiftly it may fall down the precipice of falsehood" (*Rambler* no. 104, 4:193). The same purpose is served by other abstract subjects such as begin sentences in the phrases "He who," "Such are," "There is," and "Some there are." "He that resigns his peace to little casualties, and suffers the course of his life to be interrupted by fortuitous inadvertencies, or offences, delivers himself up to the direction of the wind, and loses all that constancy and equanimity which constitute the chief praise of a wise man" (*Rambler* no. 112, 4:235). Where subordinate clauses do not prolong suspense by introducing qualifications and discriminations in mid-sentence, they can be used at the end of the sentence to delay and fortify the appearance of the most stinging thought, as in the sentence last quoted ("all that constancy and equanimity which constitute the chief praise of a wise man"). The net result of these techniques, when combined in a paragraph, or a sentence of paragraph length, is to accommodate a severity of expression that is almost painful. It must be admitted that Johnson's prose aspires to climb steadily and chillingly downward to the heart of darkness.

> At our entrance into the world, when health and vigour give us fair promises of time sufficient for the regular maturation of our schemes, and a long enjoyment of our acquisitions, we are eager to seize the present moment; we pluck every gratification within our reach, without suffering it to ripen into perfection, and crowd all the varieties of delight into a narrow compass; but age seldom fails to change our conduct; we grow negligent of time in proportion as we have less remaining, and suffer the last part of life to steal from us in languid preparations for future undertakings, or slow approaches to future advantages, in weak hopes of some fortuitous occurrence, or drowsy equilibrations of undetermined counsel: whether it be that the aged, having tasted the pleasures of man's condition, and found them delusive, become less anxious for their attainment; or that frequent miscarriages have depressed them to despair, and frozen them

to inactivity; or that death shocks them more, as it advances upon them, and they are afraid to remind themselves of their own decay, or to discover to their own hearts, that the time of trifling is past. (*Rambler* no. 111, 4:227)

Johnson privileges the moment of tragic revelation, the "discovery" to one's own heart. But what he tends to find in his own heart in moments of revelation and discovery are the words and the resonance of literature. He is fully aware of this phenomenon, and of its strangeness.

Haunting Words

To Boswell, August 27, 1775:

> Never, my dear Sir, do you take it into your head that I do not love you; you may settle yourself in full confidence both of my love and my esteem; I love you as a kind man, I value you as a worthy man, and hope in time to reverence you as a man of exemplary piety. I hold you as Hamlet has it, "in my heart of heart," and therefore, it is little to say, that I am,
>   Sir, Your affectionate humble servant . . . (2:267)

"I hold you as Hamlet has it, 'in my heart of heart'": the quotation is from an anomalous moment in the third act of *Hamlet*, when, as they are awaiting the catastrophic event of the play-within-the-play, Hamlet turns to Horatio with this pressingly frank avowal:

> Give me that man
> That is not passion's slave, and I will wear him
> In my heart's core, ay, in my heart of heart,
> As I do thee.
>   (3.2.71–74)

The suddenness, the plangent urgency of this declaration, comes not only from legitimate, if sightly hysterical, tension but from that foreboding that is affianced to the death wish. Hamlet is putting his affairs in order in matters of the heart. He speaks with the intensity of the imaginarily doomed, as, in a more sustained dramatization of this peculiar affect, Antony does on the night before the second battle of Actium. After feasting his friends and servants, he reduces them to tears with his perturbed farewell and his somber affirmation: "I look on you / As one that takes his leave" (4.2.28–29). When Johnson quotes Hamlet's phrase, it is with the same deep finality with which Hamlet speaks it, made even deeper by the act of quotation—this strange self-occlusion at the heart of heart, in which the words of another substitute for one's own.[7]

Johnson's sense of the resonance of literature can be gathered from the use of quotation in this and similar passages from his personal correspondence (all from *Letters*). He seems at least on the surface to divide literature between a secularized, eroticized friend to life and a dark, quasi-sacred antagonist to it. As we have already observed, many of Johnson's quotations place literature directly on the side of solitude and death. He persistently makes use of his literary memory to prefigure his own end, as when he sees before him "Johnson's *grimly ghost*" (4:188) or the days when, as "Colin," he will be "forgotten and gone" (3:67). In this vein, he borrows frequently from Swift's bitterly longsighted poem "The Death of Dr. Swift." He even identifies with the ill-fated Dido, whom we last saw him contemptuously dismissing when Aeneas has abandoned her and she grieves in nightmares of lonely drifting. "I have not been so well for two years past. The great malady is neither heard, seen, felt, nor—understood. But I am very solitary." And, quoting Virgil, he adds, "'Semperque relinqui / Sola sibi, semper longam incomitata videtur / Ire viam'" [She always finds herself alone, abandoned, / and wandering without companions on / an endless journey—*Aen.* 4:466, Mandelbaum trans. 99] (4:232). Literature intervenes here as the voice of doom, the Stone Guest who has come to proclaim the will of fate. It makes a still more dramatic intervention with the italicized quotation from the following passage—a quotation untraced, but as solemn and authoritative as scripture: "We have run this morning twenty four miles, and could run forty eight more. *But who can run the race with Death?*" (4:358).

By contrast, other of Johnson's quotations identify literature with the return to life. Thus in rejecting anxiety about his sickness and its future, he finds occasion to quote Martial: "I come home, I think, worse than I went; and do not like the state of my health. But *vive hodie,* make the most of life. I hope to get better, and—sweep the cobwebs" (3:92). Here Johnson's quotation assimilates literature to "the living world," which he pursues with certain sadness and determined gaiety. When the two equally urgent voices of literature speak in alternation, the contrast between them is made vivid: "But alas, I had no sleep last night, and sit now panting over my paper. *Dabit Deus his quoque finem.* [Even to this God will grant an end.] I have really hope from Spring, and am ready like Almanzor to bid the Sun *fly swiftly* and *leave weeks and months behind him* (4:275; Almanzor is the romantic lead in Dryden's *Conquest of Granada*). Here the Latin tag enters with superegoistic authority to give a stern, chastening reminder of death, while Dryden's words provide the terms for turning gratefully back toward "the living world."

Johnson does often use quotation in this second mode—to sustain the sense of the liminal moment and its fragile continuance. So with his quotations from Milton: "I am not yet willing to forsake *towred cities* or to leave the *busy hum of men* quite behind me" (4:178); "The time of year is not very favourable to excursions. I thought myself above assistance or obstruction from the seasons, but find the autumnal blasts sharp and nipping and the fading world an uncomfortable prospect. Yet I may say with Milton that I do not *abate* much of *heart or hope*" (3:368). This use most frequently lights upon Shakespeare, as we would expect, and in particular Shakespeare's Falstaff, everywhere a favorite embodiment of besieged and irrepressible life:

> I think that I am much more unwieldy and inert than when I was here last; my Nights are very tedious. But a light heart etc. ["A light heart lives long," *Love's Labor's Lost* 5.2.18] (3:49)
>
> I am old, I am old, says Sir John Falstaff. (3:77)
>
> Did you see Foote at Brighthelmstone—Did you think he would so soon be gone? Life, says Falstaff, is a shuttle. (3:92)
>
> I have thus *ended* for the present *joy and woe* and we may now *talk a little like folks of this world* (4:220; via Prior's "A Better Answer

(To Chloe Jealous)": "Pr'ythee quit this Caprice; and (as old FALSTAFF says) / Let Us e'en talk a little like Folks of This World").

In these passages Johnson turns to literature as to the restoration of life and the refuge from death, yet this use of quotation does not in the end succeed in distinguishing itself from that earlier, more forbidding application. Johnson aligns literature with eros, but it is an ambiguous and shadowed eros, one that emphasizes not the hardiness but the pathos of the living. The quotation—both what is quoted and the act of quoting—allows Johnson to launch into a haunted bravado. This is the stance of one alone and on the edge, in a precarious, dramatic moment whose appearance of drama is sustained by the heroic turn to verse. In this way the embrace of life gathers up anxiety and gains an edge of fervor and ultimacy. Even Falstaff's exuberance is darkened when Johnson chooses to quote him echoing Job's lament, "My days are swifter than weaver's shuttle, and are spent without hope." Literature gives a voice to grim necessity and, at the same time, to that which flees from it, to eros. But by means of the ultimacy of quotation—the ultimacy of Hamlet's phrase "heart of heart"—these voices express the same fatefulness. In Johnson's use of it, the ultimacy of quotation—its resonance as of a voice from the threshold—guarantees that eros will express the fatality that haunts it. The grandeur of literary language is fitted to speak most eloquently for last and final things.

What is it about literary experience that generates this sense of ultimacy in quotation? Every act of quotation seems to evoke the pathos of the living, the sense that the present world is fragile by comparison with the floating authority of books. This affect turns out, strangely enough, to be at one with the love of mimesis; it is the mimetic representation of the world that inspires our tenderness for it and makes it seem frail and tremulous, as if *it* were the reflection in the mirror. Through the love of mimesis, an archaic fixation and an unsatisfiable longing, literature stimulates a nostalgia for humanity and at the same time a nostalgia for literature. We have seen how Johnson chaffed against representation for not sustaining the mimetic mode powerfully enough and how he secretly missed the child's deep and delighted acceptance of literary illusion. The love of mimesis is doomed to become the nostalgia for mimesis, a nostalgia that renders the "living world" itself a perpetual disappointment, a weak imitation of imitation that can only rekindle interest by way of its poverty. The "beauty of the world" Weil hungered for was similarly frail and similarly fit to be elegized. The love of mimesis empties experience out and so transforms itself into a source of mourning. As Walter Benjamin wrote, "For someone who is past experiencing, there is no consolation" (184).

The autonomy of quotations, and therefore of literary memory, sustains the sense of tenuousness in the experiential world. The immutability of quotations grants them a unique authority; they offer a commanding, even forbidding account of inchoate experience, which comes to seem frail and unsure by comparison. In a letter written to Mrs. Thrale near the sudden, unexpected end of their friendship, Johnson finds himself involuntarily reminded of Pope's dark imaginings, and he immediately makes the application to himself: "I read your last kind letter with great delight, but when I came to *love* and *honour,* what sprang in my Mind?—How lov'd, how honour'd once, avails thee not" (from Pope's "Elegy to the Memory of an Unfortunate Lady"; 4:187). Here Johnson's postexperiential fatalism—a fatalism, that is, that seems to speak from above and beyond life—makes its literary influence vividly apparent. The words of the quotation recur as if automatically, "springing" up in the mind, to cast their judgment on experience, to cast a shadow over it. They prophesy that their immutable truth will be eternally reenacted: its temporary avatar is to be Johnson's own life.

Johnson affirmed this "stability" of truth; but seen thus, its stability—its repetition, in words and experience—is an ambivalent phenomenon whose appearance of inevitability, moreover, owes something to the contagious power of literary quotation. To have incorporated the words of literature, to have them at your heart's core, enables you to think that the truth is a thing, compact, substantial, and incorporable. "Truth indeed is always truth, and reason is always reason; they have an intrinsick and unalterable value, and constitute that intellectual gold which defies destruction" (*Lives* 1:49). The "intellectual gold" is the gold of literary language, so impressive and memorable that it lends its materiality to the appearances of truth.

But the words of literature are floating and haunting; they come and go as if at their own volition, according to some unfamiliar form of the will, without full consciousness. It is this other volition that literature seems to whisper to us, in its uncanny echoes and returns. These are what we take for intimations of the character of fate. For Johnson and other modern readers, literature in its apparent independence and commanding permanence seems to speak for chilling, invisible, indifferent laws. Fate is the suprapersonal truth that our life harbors, as the mind harbors the alien memory of words. Thus literary language can communicate the inhuman autonomy of fate. The sources of literature's power—its mimetic appearances, its generality, its iterability, and its inclination toward pathos—combine to foster the conception of a truth aligned with severity and sadness. Literature creates the "stability" of truth and makes it synonymous with fatality. Yet in Johnson's case, what should this dark power do but make literature more familiar and more susceptible of transference, or to put it another way, more beloved? October 25, 1784: "The town is my element, there are my friends, there are my books to which I have not yet bidden farewel, and there are my amusements" (4:428).

CHAPTER 4

Daimonic Splendor

On the face of it, there are nothing but differences between Johnson and Shelley—differences in era; in temperament and taste; in life and character; and in almost every literary, intellectual, and political position. There remains the one significant relation between them—that both were drawn to the ideas and styles of the tragic sense—but even so, their fascination did not take the same form. While the manifestations of Johnson's belief in the tragic paradigm were remarkably stable and consistent, Shelley had an intricate, vexed relation to the principle of the truth's cruelty, or rather he had a range of relations to it—experimental, participatory, critical, and (in some ways consciously, in others unconsciously) accepting. Shelley's involvement in the tragic paradigm was not steady and unquestioned but conscious and complex. In all his intellectual acuity, he was moved—though not without ambivalence—by the idea that a searching mind must take demystification as its project and thereby be doomed to disillusionment. Yet this sense of the necessity for a skeptic disposition was clearly at odds with another strain in Shelley—a determinedly cooperative and perfectionist strain, sometimes called the "visionary," by which he sought to encourage "love, admiration, trust and hope," in the words of *Prometheus Unbound*. This tendency of personality or intellect was of course less vivid in Johnson, so that with all its attendant consequences in literary, philosophical, and political attitudes, it makes the distinction between them; it provoked Shelley's struggle with the conviction of the truth's grimness, a struggle in which Johnson does not much share. Shelley's case is in this respect more subtle than Johnson's.

It is a commonplace of Shelley criticism to attribute to him a grave conflict of perspectives and a continual vacillation between some species of pessimism and some species of resistance to it. This conflict is sometimes described as a contest between his skepticism and his idealism, though the meaning of both those terms, and especially the term "skepticism," varies from critic to critic. The strain of criticism initiated by C. E. Pulos argues that Shelley was a skeptic of the tentative Socratic variety, which would suspend confidence in the reliability of our knowledge. In this view, Shelley's skepticism amounts to a refusal of decision, to a stance of determined and principled doubt. Pulos was followed in his line of argument by Lloyd Abbey and Earl Wasserman, though Wasserman complicated the interpretation by adding that Shelley was particularly torn between "contradictory desires for worldly perfection and an ideal postmortal eternity" (ix). Many critics have remarked on the more general conflict between "Utopianism" and some form of disillusionment in Shelley (whether it is despair only of this world or of transcendental ideals as well).

In another interpretation, it was Shelley's skepticism that led to his very disillusionment. Under this definition, the skeptical Shelley was the tough-minded realist: his skepticism was the authentic form of his intelligence, and as he matured, it compelled him to repudiate his Utopianism, along with the other "naive" ideals of his earlier poetry. This is the sense of skepticism in which it is identified with intellectual independence, critical acumen, circumspection, and subtlety. It is credited especially with resistance to sentimentality and to reassuring or comfortable illusion. The poststructuralist Shelley exhibits this form of skepticism, for which he is praised. In Bloom's analysis, Shelley met with disillusionment as the price of insight. In contrast, both Paul de Man in "Shelley Disfigured" and Tilottama Rajan in *Dark Interpreter* argue against the simple notion that the more Shelley advanced in understanding and experience, the more disillusioned he became. Yet even in their account, his poems still reflect discouraging insight and increase in it over time. For disillusionment is recombined with epistemological skepticism in this deconstructive analysis: it is said that in his last poems Shelley—or his work—came to endorse the de Manian rejection of the promises of knowledge.[1]

Both of these two general interpretations of Shelley's skepticism have the merit of reasserting his philosophical rigor and subtlety. They have succeeded in offering an antidote to the exaggeration of the visionary in Shelley. I accept some of their conclusions or at least can be said to move within the ambit of their general view. And in a sense I do not go beyond the claim for a perpetual vacillation or conflict in Shelley between the magnetism of a despairing view and its determined repudiation. But I do not think that this struggle was only or primarily philosophical and psychological; instead, it reflects Shelley's ambivalent relation to a standard of literary power, which he was drawn to, and drawn to aspire after, in spite of sporadic resistance. Pulos and his followers, who interpret Shelley's skepticism as determined philosophical doubt, are compelled to omit or temper Shelley's peculiar poetic intensity and strength of aspiration. Theirs is in some ways a rather improbable and esoteric Shelley. It is rare (even in Wasserman, who is an attentive close reader) that the literary affect and literary ambition of Shelley's poems are felt in these critics' accounts. The poststructuralist Shelley has a more immediate literary appeal, but precisely for a reason that ought to be in question. The skepticism of this Shelley already participates in the tragic paradigm: the intellectual strength of his poetry is seen to flow from disillusionment—even in the case of the deconstructive analysis, where disillusionment may not belong to Shelley himself but is in any case required of us. For epistemological skepticism, too, demands the surrender of "enabling" assumptions, pleasures, and assurances in favor of the unwelcome truth.

Shelley was undoubtedly a skeptic in the widest sense, as was Johnson, despite his disdain for both religious and philosophical skepticism—that is, despite those very conservative habits of thought that make him seem so much the antithesis of Shelley. Johnson makes a point of denying and deflating what he sees as pleasurable and what we now call enabling illusions. Shelley sometimes attacks illusions related to sanguine innocence on the one hand or to blindness and prejudice on the other; but sometimes he defends the sources of hope from the charge that they are illusory. Johnson's skeptic disposition most commonly reveals itself in the course of argument with his listeners, his reader, or himself; it is the principle of suspicion by which he brings us up short, challenges our complacency, denies us our consolations, and so forth. In Shelley, the spirit of skepticism issues in an Oedipal rebelliousness of all sorts, and ultimately in questioning of the intellectual, social, and political status quo. He was, or prided himself on being, rigorously iconoclastic. (Naturally, he rejected a good deal of his eighteenth-century heritage, including Johnson, whom he characterized as one of "the thousand narrow bigots educated in the bosom of classicality" [*Letters* 1:316]).

The difficulty is that this skeptical definition of the project of intelligence, and this sense of the locus of literary power, committed Shelley in advance to the tragic paradigm, whose authority and conclusions he often wished to reject. There is inherently a relation between skepticism, taken in the broader sense, and the notion of the grimness of the truth—that is, the notion that the truth to be revealed will be undesirable, wounding, or in Johnson's precise language, "contrary to our wishes." Shelley's mixture of iconoclasm and literary ambition automatically inclined him to the tragic paradigm. Indeed, from the very beginning, Shelley can be seen to have searched for ideas and elements of style that would fulfill the paradigm of the truth's grimness. He had always been fascinated by the overarching, bird's-eye view—Johnson's "wide survey"—with which the projects of intelligence seem so seductively identified. And it is this kind of supramundane perspective that makes possible the stunningly dark generalizations of *Adonais* and *The Triumph of Life*. As I have implied in earlier chapters and will seek to show more explicitly in this one, the generalizing project has an internal attraction to grimness. Generalization itself exerts a formal pressure toward concision and severity. For Shelley the tragic paradigm came to be sustained by the attractions of a rhetorical sharpness, akin to Johnson's, in which he grew more and more proficient. His powers grew phenomenally in the four years before his death, but the very technical expertise he gained was especially suited to evoking the grimness of the truth; it was precisely the severe style at which he came to excel. Yet the very intensity to which he always aspired bears within it a bias to tragedy; and so even Shelley's characteristic "eroticism" emerges as a strangely radiant avatar of his skeptical disappointment. The passionate features of Shelley's poetics—lushness, longing, and a certain species of exuberance—are themselves made to serve the purposes of a bleak perspective.

Daimonic Splendor

Debates on the nature and power of Shelley's skepticism naturally focus on *The Triumph of Life,* that poem which strangely combines despair and poetic splendor and is therefore treated as the acme of Shelley's "negative knowledge." It is commonly imagined that Shelley simply came to believe in the grimness of the truth as he got older. He is thought to have begun in youthful idealism and to have traveled along a fateful curve downward to disillusionment. On the surface, it does look as if all of Shelley's changes settled down into despair and he stumbled upon a willed or at least welcome death—as if, that is, the grimness of the truth had taken hold of his mind and determined the events of his life. This is a chill though tempting thought for us, since it would seem to confirm the authority of the tragic paradigm and to support those adumbrations of literature's priority over life that Johnson, for one, came to believe in. But this notion of priority suggests too neat a picture—it is probably incoherent or tautological as well—and it has to be repudiated. Shelley's writing did not dictate his life, and to think that it did is to fall under the sway of the tragic paradigm.

Rending the Veil

Any skeptical unveiling of the world is inherently ambiguous, since it can mean the unveiling either of a numinous reality or of the reality of nothingness. The word "skepticism" accordingly ranges in meaning from doubt about the certainty or even the possibility of knowledge to annihilating dismissal of what passes for mundane reality. Skepticism begins, in any case, by claiming to furnish that wide survey that Wittgenstein calls "perspicuous representation." Wittgenstein suggested that "the concept of a perspicuous representation is of fundamental significance for us. It earmarks the form of account we give, the way we look at things." Thought promises us a "clear view of things" ("übersichtlich" is the word translated as "perspicuous"), and we in turn think it possible to command a full view of whatever thought takes as its object. "Perspicuous representation" gives an overview, and thus it is conceptually linked to the ideals of objectivity, comprehensiveness, and authoritative generalization—in short, to that extensive, even superhuman power of sight Johnson associated with a "wide survey." This is to say that it has an ideological element; perspicuous representation privileges a certain way of seeing things. Wittgenstein appears to have recognized that ideological element: following his account of perspicuous representation, he asks, "Is this a Weltanschauung?" (*Philosophical Investigations* no. 122). He was wondering, I take it, if esteem for overviews of the world does not already constitute or entail a "world-view."[2] For the ideal of perspicuous representation contains a bias in favor of the distant, impersonal, and abstract: the view of one detached from individuality and removed from the world. It is therefore an element in or a precondition for the severity of generalization in Johnson as well as for the loftiness of both epistemological skepticism and the skeptic disposition.

The flight over the earth and the heavens, one of Shelley's governing poetic ideas, realizes in physical form the claims of perspicuous representation. To take a relatively neutral example of this idea, there is the ascension of Queen Mab's chariot in canto one of *Queen Mab*; it rises over the oceans, past the clouds, and beyond the sun:

> The magic car moved on.
> Earth's distant orb appeared
> The smallest light that twinkles in the heaven.
> Whilst round the chariot's way
> Innumerable systems rolled,
> And countless spheres diffused
> An ever-varying glory.
>
> (canto 1:249–55)[3]

Shelley was partial to this exhilarating fantasy of space travel, which he might have learned to like in *Paradise Lost*. A similar but somewhat lower flight is taken by the cloud, the skylark, the West Wind, and the second of the two spirits in the poems that bear their names. In *Hellas*, it is Victorious Wrong who gains this bird's-eye view on her descent toward earth, her prey. The chorus of captive Greek women describes Wrong pausing over the vast scene, on the verge of polluting it:

> I saw her, ghastly as a tyrant's dream,
> Perch on the trembling pyramid of night

> Beneath which earth and all her realms pavilioned lay
> In visions of the dawning undelight.
>
> (942–45)

This image of anthropic flight readily combines with the purposes of Shelley's skepticism, since the identification of night as a "pyramid" (or "cone") and of Heaven as a "canopy" or "pavilion" does the work of suggesting their limitedness and the unknown magnitude of what lies beyond them.

Shelley's "Ode to Heaven" follows the skeptical logic inherent in these metaphors. Apostrophizing Heaven as the "Palace-roof of cloudless nights, / Paradise of golden lights," an anonymous celebrant flies out to the limit of the Heavens and looks back to see the planets, moons, and stars in their dance:

> Glorious shapes have life in thee—
> Earth and all Earth's company
>   Living globes which ever throng
>   Thy deep chasms and wildernesses
>   And green worlds that glide along.
>
> (10–14)

To this atheistic naturalist, human beings are the byword of evanescence: "Their unremaining Gods and they / Like a river roll away—Thou remainest such alway" (25–27). But "A Remoter Voice" intervenes to take the idealist position that the Heavens are the evanescent apparition, doomed to fade in the higher reality of the ultimate, beyond "the portal of the grave" (32). A paradoxically "Louder and Still Remoter Voice" has the last word, arriving at the most distant perspective, in which both people and the Heavens are the lightest motes of a radically expanded reality:

> What is Heaven? a globe of dew
> Filling in the morning new
>   Some eyed flower whose young leaves waken
>   On an unimagined world

> Constellated suns unshaken,
> Orbits measureless, are furled
>   In that frail and fading sphere
>   With ten million gathered there
>   To tremble, gleam and disappear!—
> 					(46–54)

This perspective, which by its position in the poem promises omniscience, dismisses to oblivion all the realities to which the other voices gave authority. With this ascendence toward ever higher overviews of reality, the "Ode to Heaven" brings out how much skepticism depends on the trope of perspicuous representation. At the same time, the poem's exhilarating widening of perspective makes manifest an internal logic of skepticism—its tenacity, its contagion, and its strange demand for self-transumption. In professing its final authority, each voice teases into being a more boldly annihilating position.

"Death is the veil which those who live call life," says the ambiguous Earth of *Prometheus Unbound* (3.3.113). Figures of the veil and its rending accommodate Shelley's demand for perspicuous representation, with its consequent series of annihilations, and yet those figures are delicate and provisional to the point of obscurity. There are layers, perhaps endless layers, of veils, each of whose rendings invokes the drama of perspicuous representation. Trusting to the authority that such a representation will have over his mind, the Furies who torment Prometheus claim to expose to him the hopelessness of people's lives:

> A Fury
> Tear the veil!
>
> Another Fury
> It is torn!
>
> Chorus
> The pale stars
> Shine on a misery dire to be borne.
> 					(1.538–40)

There follows a gruesome catalogue of the forms and sources of suffering, which leaves Prometheus in despair, lamenting, "Ah woe! Alas! pain, pain ever, forever" (634–35). But the end of act one suggests that, though the Furies' abysmal description of the world was not mistaken, it had veiled another reality, the noble possibilities embodied in "those subtle and fair spirits / Whose homes are the dim caves of human thought" (659–60). In Shelley, as elsewhere, unveiling is contagious. The dramatic gesture of unveiling always makes itself vulnerable to its own unveiling as a veil. Each unveiling must profess to be ultimate at the same time that, by the imperative of ultimacy, it calls forth its own supersession. Nevertheless, in spite of his insight into this self-defeating logic, Shelley did not abandon the attractions of perspicuous representation and in fact pursues it with the greatest energy in his last poems. The rending of the veil underlies the concluding lines of *Adonais,* in which the elegist, drifting toward suicide, beholds that "the massy earth and sphered skies are riven!"

It seems that perspicuous representation bends by some inner weight toward grim revelation. Skepticism exposes the putative grounds of reality as a veil or screen of illusion. But once it begins exposing chimeras, it seems condemned to go on exposing chimeras, tearing away the veil of still more fundamental grounds. The summoning up of a supramundane vision tends by some inner necessity to accelerating skepticism or nihilistic dismissal. The "wide survey" promised at the opening of "The Vanity of Human Wishes" is, naturally, a survey of misery. Nor is anyone surprised to find that the exhilarating flights of "Ode to Heaven" should end in the bleak otherworldliness of *Adonais:* "Heaven's light forever shines, Earth's shadows fly; / Life, like a dome of many-coloured glass, / Stains the white radiance of Eternity" (461–63).

Skepticism is bound to generalizations about the nature of reality, and by its logic of exposure and contagious self-transuming, it seems bound as well to the premise that the truth it is constrained to reveal will be cruel. It must be something we will take to heart—something surprising, shocking, and to be shocking, hurtful. Conversely, the paradigm of the truth's cruelty has no life apart from perspicuous representation.

Generalization itself is a means and mode of such a representation, but one whose rhetorical form exerts its own attraction toward severity. A sovereign finality is entailed in the requirement for condensation, definitiveness, and sharp persuasive force. This is quite vivid in the case of Johnson's prose style. Surprisingly, in Shelley it is the lyric that exemplifies the charm of generalization and its consequences. Wherever his lyrics interact with the anonymous forms of wisdom literature—with proverbs and aphorisms—they join in the sweeping designs of perspicuous representation. The first two stanzas of the 1821 lyric that Mary Shelley entitled "Mutability" consist entirely of succinct and violent apothegms:

> The flower that smiles today
>   Tomorrow dies;
> All that we wish to stay
>   Tempts and then flies;
> What is this world's delight?
> Lightning, that mocks the night,
>   Brief even as bright.
>
> Virtue, how frail it is!—
>   Friendship, how rare!—
> Love, how it sells poor bliss
>   For proud despair!
> But these though soon they fall
> Survive their joy, and all
>   Which ours we call.—

This poem makes manifest the tugging within generalization to darken itself, as it works toward a conclusion whose bleakness supersedes that of the laments leading up to it. The sources of joy die, but only after having outlived joy itself. This escalation of despairing summaries echoes the technique of self-transumption that energizes skepticism. But it is more than an echo: the conjunction brings out the strange interdependence of these particular rhetorical and conceptual forms—poetic demands for sublimity and closure find an ally in critical intelligence, doubt, and disappointment.

The power of self-transumption finds another concise example in a strong late lyric, ostensibly personal rather than formulaic, whose darkness lies in catastrophic generalization, the disappearance of the individual into the shadow of the aphorism and the law:

> When passion's trance is overpast,
> If tenderness and truth could last
> Or live—whilst all wild feelings keep
> Some mortal slumber, dark and deep—
> I should not weep, I should not weep!
>
> It were enough to feel, to see
> Thy soft eyes gazing tenderly . . .
> And dream the rest—and burn and be
> The secret food of fires unseen,
> Could thou but be what thou hast been!
>
> After the slumber of the year
> The woodland violets reappear;
> All things revive in field or grove
> And sky and sea, but two, which move
> And form all others—life and love.—

The rhythm of the death of love is folded into the inexorable rhythm of the earth. Yet this reduction, with its finality and impersonality, has a darkness not quite identical with the theme of the death of love. The severity of the fiercely sweeping word "all" (all things, all others) exerts an autonomous rhetorical magnetism. The charms of generalization have here exerted themselves through a strange logic, since it is in the absence of life that things "revive." Totalized entities confront one another in a mutually exclusive relation. "All things" survive but life and love—which are all, in another sense. The structure of this ironic reduction has an authority independent of its subject. Shelley seeks out the resonance of sweeping finality here, as Johnson did when he uttered his proclamation

"No man ever wrote, except for money." Whatever the terms in which they filled it out, Shelley's poems pursued this reduction again and again. From *Alastor* through "Stanzas written in Dejection," *Julian and Maddalo, The Cenci, Adonais,* and *The Triumph of Life,* it is as if dark generalization had to go in search of its content. Thus these two lyrics enact in small the self-transuming and self-consuming itineraries, not only of many longer Shelley poems, but of his career as a whole.

Resisting the Tragic Paradigm

Shelley was apparently bound by an imperative to rend the veil and discover the ever more sublime, discouraging truth. But to the same extent that he was bound by this imperative, he was, like Wittgenstein, suspicious of so strong and reflexive a demand in himself, especially because it appeared to have political and ideological consequences he opposed. Shelley was vigorous in his skeptical attitude toward received ideas, and this involved him in the work of demystification; yet he also saw demystification as a destructive principle, and he wanted fearlessly to embrace the idealism that demystification is condemned to regard as naive. In this way he deliberately set himself against the prestige of skepticism and the authority of negation. A number of his middle works take this contest as their subject, seeking to undermine that bias in favor of the dark view that Shelley shrewdly perceived to be somehow automatic. He understood, moreover, that this bias was in some way corroborated by the tendencies of literature, for he saw himself as engaged in a deliberate effort to reform literary tastes or to recreate the mode of literary power. He meant specifically to redirect the emotions of the lyric and invent new possibilities for the literary sublime. He undertook this task in earnest with *Prometheus Unbound,* defended it theoretically in "The Defense of Poetry," and elaborated on it in lyrics such as "The Two Spirits: An Allegory."

"The Two Spirits" allegorizes the conflict between skeptical mistrust and "naive" confidence, between the severe and the buoyant. That is clear enough; but because he has represented this conflict in the form of a dialogue, Shelley has portrayed it specifically as a rhetorical struggle, a contest to see which state can figure itself most impressively or best accommodate the requirements for literary power. The first spirit epitomizes the rhetorical authority of demystification and grimness. It cautions the second spirit against aspiration, foretelling doom from the inevitable frustration of desire. It manifests its "realistic sorrow and wisdom"[4] as it warns the second spirit, "A shadow tracks thy flight of fire— / Night is coming!" (3–4). The second spirit's rhetoric is that of an erotic and imaginative sublime. It proclaims its brave, determined expectation: "If I should cross the shade of night / Within my heart is the torch of love / And that is day" (10–12). The spirit affirms that it will not be overtaken by night and storm, by fear and disillusionment, because its own conviction and strength will survive to counteract them; the "calm within and the light around" will "make night day." The second spirit clearly has the harder time of it, argumentatively, since it must resort to such improbable formulas, such complex high rhetoric, as this, while the first spirit speaks an easier language. On the other hand, the second spirit sharply undermines the magistry of the first's fatalism, representing it as a mask for sluggishness and imaginative poverty or for mere stubborn pessimism: "Thou when the gloom is deep and stark / Look from thy dull earth slumberbound / My moonlike flight thou then mayst mark" (29–31).

The two spirits' contest is not decisive in itself. Their dialogue is followed by two stanzas that present naturalized versions of the spirits' claims. Yet the poem closes with something like the perspective of the second spirit:

> Some say when the nights are dry [and] clear
> And the death dews sleep on the morass,
> Sweet whispers are heard by the traveller
>   Which make night day—
> And a shape like his early love doth pass
> Upborne by her wild and glittering hair,
> And when he wakes on the fragrant grass
>   He finds night day.

The second spirit had proclaimed that the "light within" could "make night day." The poem ends with such a transformation, but it is a complex one; for the traveler does not *make* the night day. When he wakes in the light of day, he naturally finds that night has become day. Thus the transformation might seem unremarkable or even ironic. But it is not: that an unmiraculous reduplication has occurred does not vitiate the second spirit's claims. For though the world has not changed, the traveler's apprehension has. The poetry of revision has brought him *to imagine that which he knows,* in the words of Shelley's "Defense." The "poetry of life," called also "the light of life," is that which awakens the torpid traveler to day in "The Two Spirits": "It makes us the inhabitant of a world to which the familiar world is a chaos. It reproduces the common universe of which we are portions and percipients, and it purges from our inward sight the film of familiarity which obscures from us the wonder of our being. It compels us to feel that which we perceive, and to imagine that which we know. It creates anew the universe, after it has been annihilated in our minds by the recurrence of impressions blunted by reiteration" (*Shelley's Poetry and Prose* 505–6). Reality remains unchanged, but the traveler's relation to it has altered in such a way that he no longer construes it as the inevitable site of mediocrity, tedium, and disappointment. Now it has the potential to contain "a shape as of his early love." In this poem, Shelley exposes the ideological bias in equating knowledge and experience with disillusionment.[5]

Shelley's "Defense of Poetry" argues that poetry introduces us to this other, antitragic reality. Shelley's "Defense" seeks to unsettle the category of the aesthetic and to redefine poetry so that it takes on the most general sense. What is meant by "poetry" in this work is nothing less than the heart of possibility, the spring of all thought and interest. Rather than expressing or shaping or even creating the imagination for social change, it *is* that imagination: "There is no want of knowledge respecting what is wisest or best in morals, government, and political economy, or at least what is wiser and better than what men now practice and endure. . . . We want the creative faculty to imagine that which we know; we want the generous impulse to act that which we imagine; we want the poetry of life" (*Shelley's Poetry and Prose* 502). Poetry has this recreative force "whether it spreads its own figured curtain, or withdraws life's dark veil from before the scene of things," whether it is visionary or skeptical—as if to suggest, not wrongly, that skepticism too has at least a phase of wondrous illumination. Shelley's "Defense" would thus seem to associate the aim of poetry with the aspiring, celebratory lyricism of the second spirit. But his "Defense" is hardly proof of his "naïveté," for it was composed in the same year that he wrote such despairing works as "The Flower That Smiles Today," "When Passion's Trance Is Overpast," and *Adonais*. "The Two Spirits" and "A Defense of Poetry" belong to the aspect of Shelley in which he rejects transumptive fatalism as the criterion of superior intelligence or of truth.

It is in *Prometheus Unbound* that Shelley defied the tragic paradigm most explicitly and at the same time engineered his most innovative poetics. He wanted to align sublimity in poetry with what he calls in his preface "beautiful idealisms of moral excellence"—with goodness, benevolence, love, wonder. This was in Shelley an antitragic impulse—as in Wittgenstein—arising not only out of his commitment to political "hope" ("until the mind can love, and admire, and trust, and hope, and endure") but out of a philosophical realization, going hand and hand with his political thought, that the attractions of the paradigm of tragic necessity stand at odds with other desirable works of the intelligence. With *Prometheus Unbound,* Shelley attempted to develop a revolutionary poetics, lyrical and celebratory, that would eschew this paradigm, along with the taut, wounding irony and violence of a commanding sublime rhetoric. This attempt is allegorized in Prometheus's rejection of the curse he had leveled against Jupiter. When the Phantasm of Jupiter repeats the curse, it appears as a refreshing and emboldening return to the dramatic language of the Shakespearean, and via Satan's Shakespearean speeches, the Miltonic sublime. This burst of drum-beating couplets climaxes in the last two stanzas:

> But thou who art the God and Lord—O thou
>   Who fillest with thy soul this world of woe,
> To whom all things of Earth and Heaven do bow
>   In fear and worship—all prevailing foe!
>   I curse thee! let a sufferer's curse
>   Clasp thee, his torturer, like remorse,
>   Till thine Infinity shall be

> A robe of envenomed agony;
> And thine Omnipotence a crown of pain
> To cling like burning gold round thy dissolving brain.
>
> Heap on thy soul by virtue of this Curse
>   Ill deeds, then be thou damned, beholding good,
> Both infinite as is the Universe
>   And thou, and thy self-torturing solitude.
>   An awful Image of calm power
>   Though now thou sittest, let the hour
>   Come, when thou must appear to be
>   That which thou art internally.
> And after many a false and fruitless crime
> Scorn track thy lagging fall through boundless space and time.
>   (1:282–301)

Prometheus's audience is understandably chagrined when he repudiates this inspiring rhetoric with seemingly lame and pacific, if dignified, sentences: "It doth repent me: words are quick and vain; / Grief for awhile is blind, and so was mine. / I wish no living thing to suffer pain" (1.302–5). The Earth interprets his pacifism as rationalization, as proof that he lies "fallen and vanquished." He is in fact making a sacrifice not only of heated aggressivity and the pleasures of revenge but of a rhetorical sublimity that belongs to agonism and violence.

Prometheus here dismisses the rhetorical temptations of the tragic paradigm, but he has yet to face the deeper intellectual temptation of peremptory disillusionment. His renunciation of his curse is often interpreted as the climax of act one, since it constitutes the only "act" in act one; but the crisis actually arrives with the Furies' torture of Prometheus, for they entice him to despair of humanity, and such despair would spell the annihilation of what Prometheus represents. The Furies promise not to spare him; though physical torture may have proved its futility, there are more effective psychical tortures to choose from. The Furies mock him first for imagining he will be teased with thoughts whose emptiness he recognizes and has only to resist:

> Thou think'st we will live through thee, one by one,
> Like animal life; and though we can obscure not
> The soul which burns within, that we will dwell
> Beside it, like a vain loud multitude
> Vexing the self-content of wisest men—
> That we will be dread thought beneath thy brain
> And foul desire round thine astonished heart
> And blood within thy labyrinthine veins
> Crawling like agony.
>
> (1:483–91)

According to the Furies, Prometheus complacently dreams that they will be in him but not of him; they will only be "beside," "beneath," "around" him or bottled in his "veins." His hope and integrity (called "soul") will be easy to maintain, since what attempts to attack it will be analogous to physical torture and hence susceptible of being deflected by force of mind. He will face no real temptation to believe in the Furies' suggestions; their insistence will be simply irritating, like "a vain loud multitude / Vexing the self-content of wisest men," and requiring merely patience and fortitude to endure it.

He is not to get off so easily, they say; and they are right: the grim thoughts they inculcate at the end of the act do nearly overwhelm and disable him. They threaten him with more than the "vexation" of weak doubts and anxieties; they know how to play on his own real potential for despair (and they are, of course, nothing but this potential). The despair they promulgate is political: it is the demoralization and inertia of political reaction, which springs here from two specific political failures: the self-betrayal of Christianity and the collapse of the French Revolution. Both of these idealistic movements backfired, engendering the opposite of their Utopian promises, bringing into the world even greater tyranny, corruption, bloodshed, and suffering than that which they were originally created to resist. Christ's words, for example, "outlived him," but only in order to "[Wither] up truth, peace and pity" (1.549); with the result that now his "mild and gentle ghost / Wail[s] for the faith he kindled" (1.555). The fate of these political hopes—these efforts after improvement and change—would seem to support a classic conservative position that Albert O. Hirschman has lately analyzed under the name of "the perversity thesis," that is, the reactionary's argument that reformative efforts are futile, even dangerous, because "everything backfires," and "the attempt to push society in a certain direction will result in its moving all right, but in the opposite direction" (11).

These are the first bleak thoughts with which the Furies tease Prometheus; yet the collapse of Utopian hopes into anarchy and violence is not, they say, the blackest vision they have to depress him with: "Worse things, unheard, unseen, remain behind." The temptation now takes its most subtle but most powerful form in the Fury's splendidly dark summary of human helplessness:

> In each human heart terror survives
> The ravin it has gorged: the loftiest fear
> All that they would disdain to think were true:
> Hypocrisy and custom make their minds
> The fanes of many a worship, now outworn.
> They dare not devise good for man's estate
> And yet they know not that they do not dare.
> The good want power, but to weep barren tears.
> The powerful goodness want: worse need for them.
> The wise want love, and those who love want wisdom;
> And all best things are thus confused to ill.
>
> (1.618–28)

Here the Furies urge on Prometheus the view most damaging to his own conceptions: the notion that living itself—just living—erodes confidence and self-esteem and so defeats the individual's capacity for boldness, courage, and hope.[6] "In each human heart terror survives / The ravin it has gorged": the immediate occasion of the terrible experience may pass, but the anguish remains; and the real scar is this permanent terror, which survives its original occasion and remains tenacious even after it has become irrelevant. The real harm of anxieties and disappointments lies not in their immediate effect or their practical consequences but in their second-order effects, their emotional legacy: to intimidate one before life, discredit passion and the sense of power, deny possibility, persuade one of individual and collective helplessness.

The "loftiest" secretly fear the hopelessness of their hopes; they fear it, and thus at some level they believe it, which of course makes them anticipate their failure. Their loftiness is fractured with a hidden and silent fatalism: they shrink from their brave conceptions and surrender to tacit conviction of life's weight and intransigence. They sink their eroded self-esteem in the reassurance of collective tradition. In this way "hypocrisy and custom make their minds / The fanes of many a worship, now outworn." They have been made timorous: "They dare not devise good for man's estate / And yet they know not that they do not dare." Though the disappointments that inevitably follow from experience first challenge bolder hopes, the surrender of hope itself is never required of us; it occurs as if spontaneously, from within.

This kind of self-defeat, a mental or internal defeat, poses the ultimate threat to Prometheus. For Prometheus to see people as doomed to suffer self-defeat is for him to suffer a self-defeat of that very sort: what Rousseau in *The Triumph of Life* calls being overcome by one's own heart alone. Shelley is concerned with this vaster disappointment and its structure of internal erosion here and all the way through, from "The Two Spirits" and *Julian and Maddalo* to his last poem; it is the erosion and collapse from within, of that in us which looks forward, hopes, strives, works, wonders, burns. Shelley is not merely—not melodramatically—fascinated with this collapse but interested in it analytically. He shows how it works on itself so that it seems both arbitrary and unnecessary on the one hand and fated and intransigent on the other.

Shelley therefore sought to separate literary power from its association with tragic sense. As part of this project, he sought specifically to reinvent the sublime in an erotic but still denaturalizing and passionate mode. This is the work of the third act and even more the fourth act of *Prometheus Unbound,* acts that would otherwise seem puzzlingly prolonged, and redundant, however beautiful. Harold Bloom has helpfully written that "in Act IV the imagination of Shelley breaks away from the poet's apparent intention, and visualizes a world in which the veil of phenomenal reality has been rent, a world like that of the Revelation of St. John" (*Percy Bysshe Shelley* 10). *Prometheus Unbound* is structured as an unveiling of progressively higher realities. The scope of the play radically widens, escaping the limitations of time and human perspective. This dramatic expansion of view—the rending of veils—obeys the same skeptical imperative that generates the structure of the "Ode to Heaven": act four presents still louder and remoter voices than those in act three. At the heart of the act is the hymeneal dance of the Earth and the Moon, anthropomorphized so as to be enfolded in the ode's "frail and fading sphere." But their supernatural passion is unquestionably uncanny, as will be remembered from the Earth's notorious exclamation "It interpenetrates my granite mass" or the Moon's description of sexual awakening:

> The snow upon my lifeless mountains
> Is loosened into living fountains,
> My solid Oceans flow and sing and shine
> A spirit from my heart bursts forth,
> It clothes with unexpected birth
> My cold bare bosom: Oh! it must be thine
> On mine, on mine!
>
> Gazing on thee I feel, I know,
> Green stalks burst forth, and bright flowers grow
> And living shapes upon my bosom move:
> Music is in the sea and air,
> Winged clouds soar here and there,
> Dark with the rain new buds are dreaming of:
> 'Tis Love, all Love!
>
> (4:356–69)

This revelation of a postapocalyptic paradise provides the occasion for the exuberance of a liberated figurative language. The "thrilling life" of poetic figures stands in for the awakening of "unimagined worlds." But these science-fiction imaginings already begin again to touch on strange and chilling effects. Naturalistic representation can hold Shelley's aesthetic interest for only so long, and when it fails, it gives way to a breathtaking poetics that has reassumed ambition after sublimity's tinge of the forbidding and the uncanny. Act four does deviate from the play's humanist agenda and from Shelley's intention, but it is by way of sustained obedience to the aspirations of his elevated poetics. Though *Prometheus Unbound* has been allegorized as the flowering of Shelley's "hope," its hieratic style conspires to recombine it with the fierce rhetoric of his putatively "disillusioned" poems. Shelley's departures from tragic representation thus prove to be somewhat tentative, for a self-transuming sharpness dominates his poetry, no matter how "Utopian," celebratory, or lyrical its appearance.

Shelley waged a keen-minded and principled resistance to what he perceived as the inherent rhetorical advantage of skepticism and grimness.[7] For his struggle was not only or perhaps ever primarily an intellectual and psychological one; it was also a struggle against a literary imperative, a contest with the tragic paradigm. Shelley was trying to subvert the equation of tragic affect and sublime style with literary power. Hence he defied the automatic authority of demystification; he questioned and to some extent exposed it in works like "The Two Spirits" and *Prometheus Unbound.* Yet he was more successful at defying the assumptions of the tragic paradigm thematically than stylistically. Toward the end, this initiative largely failed in him, and there is no doubt that the events of his life and his consequent discouragement influenced this failure. But it is important to recognize how much his literary instincts worked against his noble project from the start.

At the same time that he was writing *Prometheus Unbound,* Shelley was indulging the tragic paradigm in poems like "Stanzas Written in Dejection" and *Julian and Maddalo,* two of several he sent to his publisher with the comment that they were his "saddest verses raked up into one heap." *Julian and Maddalo* contains a dramatization of the struggle between determined idealism and angry disillusionment that Shelley was entertaining. The madman's ravings provide no solution or answer to the philosophical problem, of course: after Julian and Maddalo have been to see the madman, their debate "is quite forgot" (520). Part of the poem's "sadness" may lie in this nullification of the philosophical argument, which had been "forlorn / Yet pleasing" (39–40), and has been superseded by an encounter that was forlorn without being pleasing. But the sadness of the poem colors it from the beginning and stems from the fact that Shelley does not share the hopeful perspective of his avatar in the poem, Julian. Or, to put it another way, Julian portrays his own earlier self with some degree of regretful condescension, saying, for example, "I (for ever still / Is it not wise to make the best of ill?) / Argued against despondency" (46–48). By the time the poem begins, Julian has already come to regard his old idealism as ineffective, and with an attractive modesty, he seems to grant that Maddalo's despairing views exert the greater rhetorical authority (see Maddalo's speech, lines 115–30). The sense of loss here—that is, Julian's loss of his own conviction and his acceptance of a sadder perspective—is not explicitly acknowledged. It is rather an element of the atmosphere, an unspoken regret, which betrays its influence in the gorgeous descriptions of landscape. Julian's enthusiasm has taken refuge in a consciously diminished object: an appreciation for beauties felt to be transient and unrelated to humanity.

Michael O'Neill has sensitively argued that the poem dramatizes the struggle between the two competing ideologies without taking a stand; according to this view, the poem is in fact concerned to analyze the psychological situation that gives rise to such a struggle. Earl Wasserman agrees that no one wins the argument:

> The result is a poetic psychomachy that, without gaining any clear victory, uncovers for honest conscious confrontation the subliminal conflict in the poet's mind and reassures that, since at least the psychic battle has been frankly waged, the optimism of *Prometheus Unbound* is in good faith.... Shelley interrupted the composition of *Prometheus Unbound* to grapple with reality and earn for himself—at the price of much self-searching and many concessions—a hard-won and insecurely held footing in the actual human condition on which to sustain the idealism of which he had been writing in his lyric drama. (74)

Both of these readings, though subtle and attractive, depend on denying Shelley's characterization of the poem as one of his saddest. Count Maddalo may not prevail in the abstract argument, but the poem ends up confirming his affect. We are left with some resonant tragic sense, as Julian presents his fond but melancholy recollections. What Shelley appears to be doing in this poem is not "grappling with reality" as a means to justify the "idealisms" of *Prometheus Unbound* but reflecting on the magnetism of the tragic view—on its rhetorical and psychological attraction, which he had tried to combat in his play but suspected rightly was too strong for him, and his imaginings.

The Janus-faced Sublime

For Shelley, as for Weil and Johnson, the style of ancient Greek poetry presented a model literature for the grimness of the truth. The poetry of *Prometheus Unbound* follows Greek poetry, of which Shelley was a great admirer, in that its intensity arises from the denseness of its figurations. Figurative language does not recede before mimetic representation for the sake of literary affect, but rather in its fierce, obtrusive, and hieratic nature it produces its own affect. This is the same antimimetic source of drama as in Aeschylus, the dramatic question being how much pressure the language can bring to bear on itself. In taxing figuration to its limits, and more generally in treating the taxation of figures as a philosophical project, Shelley manifested a much deeper debt to Greek poetry than the superficial borrowings of his play's structure suggest. But poetry of this kind by its nature inclines toward chilling effects. These are the effects Weil discovered and treasured; they are also the effects developed, somewhat counterproductively, in the fourth act of *Prometheus Unbound*. I have argued in a previous chapter that it was this daimonized faculty, the voice of Ate or necessity, that Aeschylus captured. In Shelley, the identification of poetry with the daimonic found a willing but not unconflicted imitator, for it promoted stylistic aspirations that committed him in advance to the lofty, intimidating, and austere.

Perhaps it will seem strange to describe Shelley's poetics as austere, since his verses are full of light, color, passion, and a kind of figurative luxury. But in fact, Shelley's splendor is ambivalent, like that of Aeschylus. The Janus-faced character of the daimonic sublime governs many features of Shelley's poetry. His apostrophes and addresses, which are often startlingly novel, bring with them a vertigo that weighs on their celebratory form. Some fragments may help to recall this strangeness, since they have the virtue of unfamiliarity:

> Ye gentle visitations of calm thought—
>   Moods like the memories of happier earth
>   (*Poetical Works* 585)

> Great Spirit whom the sea of boundless thought
>   Nurtures within its unimagined caves
>   (*Poetical Works* 661)

> Thou living light that in thy rainbow hues
>   Clothest this naked world
>   (*Poetical Works* 634)

> Unrisen splendour of the brightest sun,
>   To rise upon our darkness
>   (*Poetical Works* 634)

These apostrophes invoke quite distinct and original essences, especially by comparison with the objects of conventional poetic address. Even where the objects are less unconventional, they are reanimated by an oddly intimate and individualizing perspective:

> Swiftly walk o'er the western wave,
>   Spirit of Night!

> Bright wanderer, fair coquette of Heaven,
> To whom alone it has been given
> To change and be adored forever . . .
> Envy not this dim world

> O Love, who bewailest
> The frailty of all things here

These animations have some unusual interiorizing force: it is as if poetry were speaking to itself. Other of Shelley's more famous apostrophes—to Intellectual Beauty, to Mont Blanc, to the skylark or the West

Wind—participate in this intensity of invention and separation. These are also Shelley's most accessible poems and those which have been allowed to represent his poetry—often, unfortunately, as either rhapsodic or blandly skeptical. They would profit from being reread in the context of Shelley's aspiration after eerily passionate opacity. The effect of these individualizing and intimate addresses is to heighten the anthropomorphizing character of personification, but because the essences so addressed are for the most part highly abstract and deliberately disassociated from human nature and human limitations, they seem to occupy an obscure liminal realm. The eeriness springing from this tension can be found very clearly in Shelley's apostrophes to Intellectual Beauty and to the West Wind. In both cases, though more noticeably in that of the latter, the tension between the apostrophe's anthropomorphizing and its unhumanizing ambitions is essentially the subject of the poem in that it treats the essence as daimonically double: a destroyer and a preserver. The awesomeness of semianthropomorphized essences dominates "Ode to the West Wind" from the opening stanza:

> O wild West Wind, thou breath of Autumn's being,
> Thou, from whose unseen presence the leaves dead
> Are driven, like ghosts from an enchanter fleeing....

The charm and power of the West Wind, the spirit of Intellectual Beauty, or even the Spirit of Delight in "Rarely, rarely comest thou" spring from the fact that they are beings who determine the nature of being without sharing in it. Even "The Zucca" contains a hymn to the spirit that makes everything divine: "When for a moment thou art not forbidden / To live within the life which thou bestowest" (*Poetical Works* 665). Their relation to people is for this reason uncertain, since they can be the agent of nurture and inspiration but also of violence and abandonment. Otherwise "I would ne'er have striven / As thus with thee in prayer in my sore need." This somewhat painful dynamic governs the poems to Intellectual Beauty, the Spirit of Delight, and the West Wind, whose estrangement from the speaker generates the odes or "prayers" dedicated to them. The relation of ambivalence is manifest in the near-final lines of

"Ode to the West Wind," in which the speaking subject describes himself as content to come under the canopy of unhuman power at the cost of death:

> Make me thy lyre, even as the forest is:
> What if my leaves are falling like its own!
> The tumult of thy mighty harmonies
>
> Will take from both a deep, autumnal tone,
> Sweet though in sadness. Be thou, Spirit fierce,
> My spirit! Be thou me, impetuous one!
>
> Drive my dead thoughts over the universe. . . .

The "fierceness" invoked here is that of the unhuman and unpredictable. This identification with daimonism carries over into Shelley's more designedly political poems, which take such an impersonal fierceness as the model for their polemical severity. I might choose as an example of this severity either the opening line of the sonnet "England in 1819," "An old, mad, blind, despised, and dying king," or the percussionist insistence of *The Mask of Anarchy*, an extended, suspenseful, and violent transformation of the ballad from which I quote some opening stanzas:

> I met Murder on the way—
> He had a mask like Castlereagh—
> Very smooth he looked, yet grim;
> Seven bloodhounds followed him:
>
> All were fat; and well they might
> Be in admirable plight,
> For one by one, and two by two,
> He tossed them human hearts to chew
> Which from his wide cloak he drew.
>
> Next came Fraud, and he had on,
> Like Eldon, an ermined gown;

> His big tears, for he wept well,
> Turned to millstones as they fell.
>
> And the little children, who
> Round his feet played to and fro,
> Thinking every tear a gem,
> Had their brains knocked out by them.
>
> (5–21)

The ferocity of meter and style in this passage—not least the eruptions of violence within lilting nursery rhyme—are meant to be as much mimetic of the oppression they describe as they are in themselves commanding. Anyone who beholds the misery of the times in truth will become fierce and unsentimental. Such is the antisentimentality of Shelley's "An Address to the People on the Death of Princess Charlotte" or his lines "Written on Hearing the News of the Death of Napoleon." These poems come within the orbit of grimness through their assumption of an uncanny persona and their sharpness of style. Shelley's atheistic and republican political principles joined the paradigm of truth's austerity by way of the intellectual project of skepticism. But these principles did not alter with the arc of his poetry, a fact that suggests the dubiousness of identifying his poems' intensifying tragic sense with his personal disillusionment. A feature of his style was maturing, not necessarily in tandem with other intellectual developments or the developments of his inner life.

The purposes of daimonization were served by another feature of Shelley's lyricism—the antithetical meaning of his primary words. His language of light—of brightness and splendor, and lesser and greater lights—turns out to be divalent, as does his language of darkness and night. "Bright" is a favorite token of admiration in Shelley, yet it is sometimes desirable, sometimes sinister. Prometheus, after his liberation, speaks of "the mind, arising bright / From the embrace of beauty" (3.3.50–51), while "The Invitation" addresses Jane as the "Best and brightest," and "the vessels glide / Along the ocean bright and wide" in "Lines written in the Bay of Lerici." But the word "bright" in "When the lamp is shattered" has a sharp, malevolent force: "Bright reason will mock thee." It assumes such force not because Shelley typically uses the word in this sense but because his vocabulary is composed of words hovering around deeply antithetical uses. Two other of his favorite words—"moon" and "delicate"—rotate their affect in the same way. "To Jane" praises "the moon's soft splendor," whereas "the cold chaste moon" is derided in *Epipsychidion*. In *Prometheus Unbound,* Panthea identifies for her sister Ione "the delicate spirit / That guides the earth through Heaven" (3.4.7–8), a use of "delicate" that resonates oddly with the sixth spirit's remark "Ah, sister, Desolation is a delicate thing" (1.772–73).

The most significant reversals turn on words and metaphors concerning lights and their obscuration. "Radiance" has a quite different valence in the sweet assurance "I love snow, and all the forms / Of the radiant frost" ("Rarely, rarely comest thou") from that in the fierce apothegm "Life . . . Stains the white radiance of Eternity." The use of the word "splendor" for the most intense, most powerful light provides an even more dramatic example of reversal. "Splendor" was long so admired by Shelley that he inserted it without warrant into Plato's epigram on Aster, which serves as the epigraph to *Adonais:* "Thou wert the morning star among the living, / Ere thy fair light had fled— / Now, having died, thou are as Hesperus, giving / New splendour to the dead." The poem personifies Adonais's thoughts as "Splendours" and gives to the immortal poets the name "splendours of the firmament of time" (389). But in *The Triumph of Life,* "splendor," along with many other words for light, undergoes a daimonization: the car of Life rushes forward on "the tempest of the splendour which forbade / Shadow to fall from leaf or stone" (444–45). *Hellas,* too, speaks of "the ill in splendour hid" (953), while, in "Lines Written Upon Hearing the News of the Death of Napoleon," the Earth exultingly boasts, "The dead fill me ten thousandfold / Fuller of speed, and splendour, and mirth" (26–27).

It is easy to recognize that The Triumph of Life radically and deliberately ironizes all the language of light, representing the greater lights first of the Sun and then of the chariot of Life as tyrannical effacers of shadowy beauties. Yet this was not the first time that Shelley exploited the potential for inversion in the imagery of light and darkness. "To Night" praises the darkness in terms that recall the opening stanzas of *The Triumph of Life:*

> When I arose and saw the dawn,
>   I sighed for thee;
> When light rode high, and the dew was gone,
> And noon lay heavy on flower and tree. . . .
>   (*Poetical Works*)

Night with its darkness is here the desirable time. The "shadow" whose presence, we want to say, Shelley always laments ("He has outsoared the shadow of our night") makes its own beloved appearances. In *Prometheus Unbound,* the third of the spirits of the human mind recalls of the sage's dream, "the world awhile below / Wore the shade its lustre made" (1.731–32). This shade is like the rich obscurity of the Spirit of Intellectual Beauty, "Thou—that to human thought are nourishment, / Like darkness to a dying flame," or of "Mont Blanc," the sight of which stimulates "one legion of wild thoughts, whose wandering wings / Now float above thy darkness."

Though critics sometimes assign Shelley's metaphors of lights and darkness to a fixed symbolic system, their valence is in truth migratory (with the exception of the light of Venus). The choice of this imagery is at the heart of his poetry's aspiration. For light to become radiant with dark, and darkness with light, is for it to have taken on the quality of what is "deinos," brilliantly intense and unhuman. The scheme of his colors—purple, azure, silver, and gold—is similarly daimonizing. Borrowed from Greek lyric, these colors of the treasury describe natural phenomena, yet they have their own denaturalizing force, as in this speech of Asia's in *Prometheus Unbound:* "The point of one white star is quivering still / Deep in the orange light of widening morn / Beyond the purple mountains" (2.1.17–19). This incandescence of the landscape has an uncanny effect not unlike the ascription of brilliance to darkness (and vice versa).[8]

The Eroticism of Disappointment

Severity and lushness combine strangely in Shelley's poetics. One consequence of this union is that his work brings out one feature of skepticism more vividly than Weil, Johnson, or Wittgenstein: the potential in skepticism for a kind of erotic intensity—which is another way of describing its attractions. A peculiarly ambiguous union of passion and negation characterizes Shelley's poetry. For to the skeptical theme of the world's blankness and poverty Shelley joined a strong current of eroticism—or rather, heightened a latent one. It is quite some time since F. R. Leavis criticized and traduced Shelley; his view has lost its influence, I hope, so that it will now be safe to say that his focus was sometimes well chosen, even if he went on to elaborate from it an evaluation that no longer seems convincing.[9] Leavis zeroed in on Shelley's telling revisions of "The Recollection" (Davie 87–88). The poem originated as part of "The Pine Forest of the Cascine Near Pisa," a longish lyric that Shelley divided in half to form "The Invitation" and "The Recollection." There he had described an ephemeral sensuous contentment in language that his revisions rendered atavistic:

>   A spirit interfused around,
>   A thinking, silent life;
>   To momentary peace it bound
>   Our mortal nature's strife;—
>
>   And still, it seemed, the centre of
>   The magic circle there,
>   Was one whose being filled with love
>   The breathless atmosphere.
>   (*Poetical Works*)

Leavis shrewdly identified the vocabulary of these lines as Wordsworthian, by contrast with the "characteristically Shelleyan attitude" that took their place:

>   A spirit interfused around,
>   A thrilling silent life,—
>   To momentary peace it bound
>   Our mortal nature's strife;
>   And still I felt the centre of
>   The magic circle there

> Was one fair form that filled with love
> The lifeless atmosphere.

Shelley's changes ("thrilling" for "thinking," "form" for "being," and "lifeless" for "breathless") have, as Leavis said, the effect of supercharging these lines with eroticism. To Leavis these revisions represented a culpable corruption of sensibility, but less prejudiced readers will recognize their strength. What makes them "characteristically Shelleyan" is not just eroticism but, as Leavis did not remark, the particular, ambivalent form of it—the eroticism of one lovely thing shining in darkness. This form of the erotic is inseparable from nihilism. The change from "breathless" to "lifeless" produces catastrophe. Whereas "breathless" may pass for a description of still air, "lifeless" is unmistakably fateful; it introduces the sense of phenomenality's emptiness, the death-in-life of life, which is familiar from Shelley's other late poems.

All the revisions of "The Recollection" work to intensify the poem's particular pathos of tenuous fantasy. In this way they are all eroticizing, though not in the restricted, interpersonal form that Leavis had in mind. The most interesting are the revisions of the fourth stanza, in which the reflecting pool, not mimetically exact but fruitful of beautiful mutations, makes its appearance. The draft describes the reflection as "a purple firmament of light / Which in the dark earth lay, / More boundless than the depth of night, / And clearer than the day," while the final version not only reads "purer than the day" but more subtly changes "a purple firmament of light" to "a firmament of purple light." Pools of water on a dark ground reflect a dark sky; the phrase "purple light" carries this image toward the supernatural. The natural world is transformed out of natural possibility by the properties of the reflecting medium.

Shelley constantly evokes the bleakness of this eroticism—the extent to which the strange wonder of the erotic object throws the world's poverty into relief. But it manifests itself nowhere more clearly than in the ghastly hyperboles of *Epipsychidion*:

> Seraph of Heaven! too gentle to be human,
> Veiling beneath that radiant form of Woman
> All that is insupportable in thee

> Of light, and love, and immortality!
> Sweet benediction in the eternal Curse!
> Veiled Glory of this lampless Universe!
> Thou Moon beyond the clouds! Thou living Form
> Among the Dead! Thou Star above the Storm!
>
> (21–28)

The eroticism of such a moment is a form of despair; the celebration of Emilia expresses itself in contempt for all other available reality. Many quotable passages, which are generally discussed under the rubric of Shelley's "search for the Ideal," might be cited here, but the conclusion to be drawn is evident. It is of very little importance whether or not the poetry celebrates a temporary incarnation of the Ideal; here the distinction between nihilism and affirmation is not profound.

The spectacle of the world's emptiness, which the panorama of perspicuous representation tends to produce, has special rhetorical attractions. Shelley's poetry often evokes its peculiar intensity. In this Shelley was following not only Humean skepticism but a long line of wisdom literature beginning with *Ecclesiastes*. "Lift Not the Painted Veil" both dramatizes the doomed search for what Shelley calls "love," source of "a secret correspondence with our heart" (*Shelley's Prose* 170), and treats the seeker himself as our object of love, though unregarded and lost:

> Lift not the painted veil which those who live
> Call Life; though unreal shapes be pictured there
> And it but mimic all we would believe
> With colours idly spread,—behind lurk Fear
> And Hope, twin Destinies, who ever weave
> Their shadows o'er the chasm, sightless and drear.
> I knew one who had lifted it . . . he sought,
> For his lost heart was tender, things to love
> But found them not, alas; nor was there aught
> The world contains, the which he could approve.
> Through the unheeding many he did move,
> A splendour among shadows—a bright blot
> Upon this gloomy scene—a Spirit that strove
> For truth, and like the Preacher, found it not.

This scenario of disappointment is familiar from other Shelley poems. But as framed by the directive not to lift the painted veil, it joins the tradition of wisdom literature and participates in the paradoxes of didacticism within that tradition. The poem pictures what it says we ought to be blind to and teaches what it begins by claiming we ought not to learn. The wisdom it offers is as openly useless as the insight in the aphorism from *Ecclesiastes* that Shelley used as the epigraph to his early poem "On Death": "There is nor work nor device, nor knowledge, nor wisdom, in the grave, whither thou goest." Yet this uselessness in no way vitiates the rhetorical energy of the proposition. On the contrary, it becomes for this reason impressive in the highest degree. We saw a similar phenomenon in *Rasselas*. This story of knowledge has at its heart the vigor of impermeably severe generalization.

From the prematurely defeatist *Alastor* through *The Triumph of Life*, Shelley chose perpetually to reenact the skeptical discovery of the poverty of the world, recalling the trauma of this discovery to restless life. Because skeptical disappointment is vivid only as an individual experience, he kept dramatizing it in terms of tragic awakening—as opposed to the demographical mode of Johnson's "The Vanity of Human Wishes." The seeming self-involvement of Shelley's poetry—which has been aggravating to some and licensed condescension in others—is the unfortunate consequence of Shelley's readiness to enlist the first-person, if not himself, in this wintry drama.[10]

Shelley regularly regretted the world's incapacity to saturate love or imagination. It is odd to think of this regret as itself erotic, but of course it is. In *Alastor*, Shelley had reflected on the interfluency of erotic and intellectual life—in the sense, that is, that they are the same, not metaphors for each other. From Wordsworth he had inherited the paradigm of the poet's journey as a claustrophobically solitary one, a struggle to read the mute inscriptions of nature and books. The poet is at first fortunate enough to be impressed with understanding:

> Among the ruined temples there,
> Stupendous columns, and wild images
> Of more than man, where marble daemons watch
> The Zodiac's brazen mystery, and dead men
> Hang their mute thoughts on the mute walls around,

> He lingered, poring on memorials
> Of the world's youth, through the long burning day
> Gazed on those speechless shapes, nor, when the moon
> Filled the mysterious halls with floating shades
> Suspended he that task, but ever gazed and gazed
> And gazed, till meaning on his vacant mind
> Flashed like strong inspiration, and he saw
> The thrilling secrets of the birth of time.
>
> (116–28)

It is a Wordsworthian scheme to represent the "vacant" mind waiting and straining for, or being surprised by, illumination that must come from outside (as in, for example, the Winander Boy episode or "I Wandered Lonely as a Cloud": "For oft when on my couch I lie / In vacant or in pensive mood, / They [daffodils] flash upon that inward eye / Which is the bliss of solitude"). This dynamic leaves one open to the threat that illumination will not come, which is in essence the Alastor poet's fate, as Shelley's preface describes it: "Among those who attempt to exist without sympathy, the pure and tender-hearted perish through the intensity and passion of their search after its communities, when the vacancy of their spirit suddenly makes itself felt." The difference between Shelley and Wordsworth here is that for Shelley, illumination must have erotic as well as natural and literary sources. It was Wordsworth's odd prudery in isolating erotic development that motivated this critique in *Peter Bell the Third*:

> But from the first 'twas Peter's drift
>   To be a kind of moral eunuch,
> He touched the hem of Nature's shift,
> Felt faint—and never dared uplift
>   The closest, all-concealing tunic.
>
> (313–17)

The Alastor poet perishes for want of erotic enlightenment.[11] But by the same doubling that structures "Lift Not the Painted Veil," he leaves behind a world whose deadness has only been revealed by the withdrawal of his own illuminating presence. So the final lines of the poem read:

> Art and eloquence,
> And all the shews o' the world are frail and vain
> To weep a loss that turns their lights to shade.
> It is a woe too "deep for tears," when all
> Is reft at once, when some surpassing Spirit,
> Whose light adorned the world around it, leaves
> Those who remain behind, not sobs or groans,
> The passionate tumult of a clinging hope;
> But pale despair and cold tranquillity,
> Nature's vast frame, the web of human things,
> Birth and the grave, that are not as they were.

This turn on the skeptical theme—when the disappearance of the unfulfilled lover is treated as our erotic loss—helps to bring out how it is that Shelley's gloomy poems are invested with erotic pressure. There is here an eroticism through grimness that can be found to suffuse many Shelley poems. The identification of an erotic object—lost or yet to be possessed—is not in itself so necessary; eroticism inheres in the freshness of skeptical disappointment.

Disappointment displaces eroticism without eradicating it. A diffused cathexis of the world and the threat of its withdrawal sustain eroticism, which can thus be born out of the generalizations of skeptical severity. What Leavis calls erotic in the substitution of "thrilling" for "thinking" and "lifeless" for "breathless" is just as erotic in Shelley's compellingly dark generalizations and the strong, suspenseful rhythms in which they are expressed:

> Peace, peace! He is not dead, he doth not sleep—
> He hath awakened from the dream of life—
> 'Tis we, who lost in stormy visions, keep
> With phantoms an unprofitable strife,
> And in mad trance, strike with our spirit's knife,
> Invulnerable nothings.
>
> (*Adonais* 343–48)

The distinctive ambivalence of Shelley's poetry arises from the rhetorically contradictory character of its generalizations. They are at once resplendent and severe: gorgeous in their fierceness, passionate in their disappointment. They reveal a startling feature of the language of tragic skepticism: that it harbors an almost sensual pleasure and sensual satisfaction. It is paradoxically fulfilling.

CHAPTER 5

Shelley's Fate

Shelley's strange eroticism helps to create the splendor of his late poems, for in them his version of the severe style comes to its fruition. It has been universally recognized that in his last major works, *Adonais* and *The Triumph of Life,* Shelley achieved an extraordinary combination of intellectual austerity and stylistic brilliance. But it has not been so well seen that in these late poems taken as a whole, he also betrays a self-consciousness and even an unease about his cultivation of severity. Perhaps he intuited that his increasing capacity for grimness sprang from the success of his literary ambitions: a feature of his style, and hence of the literary aspirations this style accommodated, was prevailing in his work, in some sense involuntarily. In his late poems there are traces of his alienation, separation, and oppression by a literary and intellectual imperative that was somehow exerting its autonomy from him even as he was working to fulfill it in his writing. It is, naturally, not in *Adonais* and *The Triumph of Life,* his epic works of the daimonic sublime, that these traces appear, but in his late lyrics. After recalling the stylistic virtuosity of Shelley's final long poems, this chapter will be largely devoted to exploring the shadowy resistance of the late lyrics, focusing particularly on his last, "Lines written in the Bay of Lerici," which he composed between the leaves of *The Triumph of Life.*

The Triumph of Style

Shelley knew the attractions of tragic representation well, having early in his youth written poems like "On Death" and the 1814–15 version of "Mutability": "We are as clouds that veil the midnight moon; / How restlessly they speed, and gleam, and quiver, / Streaking the darkness radiantly!—yet soon / Night closes round, and they are lost forever."[1] These first experiments in gloom appear to seek conformity with some invisible standard of literary strength. Yet how is it that Shelley, who in his adolescence was addicted to such morbid clichés, came to write persuasive and original versions of the truth's austerity?

His poetry does witness profound development of a technical order. The magnetism of certain stylistic features of the daimonic sublime brought Shelley to the nihilistic precision of *Adonais* and *The Triumph of Life*. He had grown more and more skillful at producing powerfully grim effects through a condensation of style that lends itself to irony. The foremost of these stylistic devices seems to have been the introduction of antithetical qualifiers and antithetical figures. The sonnet called "Ye hasten to the grave," whose irony is sufficiently patent in its title, offers some examples of the trenchant antithetical adjective in addressing "ye restless thoughts, and busy purposes / Of the idle brain" and asking, "O whither hasten ye, that thus ye press / With such swift feet life's green and pleasant path?" Without so much as a separate clause of explanation, "restless thoughts" and "busy purposes" are undone in their definition—as "restless" and "busy" offspring "of the idle brain." The ironies are sharp and immediate, not the subject of discursive theses but the bleakness that is already given. The high rhetoric of *Prometheus Unbound* frequently gives rise to this kind of condensation. The Furies expect Prometheus to think "that we will be dread thought beneath thy brain / And foul desire round thine astonished heart" (1.488–89). Earth praises those "who bear the untransmitted torch of hope / Into the grave across the night of life" (3.3.171–72). "The night of life," an antithetical metaphor, resembles the terms of the central ironies in *Adonais*. Just as the "foulness" that will torment Prometheus is foretold in the mention of unknown "desire," so the fact that the torch of hope will go "untransmitted" and that life is a "night" no less dark than the grave to which it leads form part of the Earth's eulogy for courage said to be vain in the breath that names it. This antithetical mode is Shelley's version of the severe style.

Such effects come to dominate his style in *Adonais* and *The Triumph of Life*, giving rise to the daimonic energy, horror, and persuasiveness of those poems:

The monsters of life's waste
        a newer band
Have pitched in Heaven's smile their camp of death

And his own thoughts, along that rugged way,
Pursued, like raging hounds, their father and their prey

Death rose and smiled, and met her vain caress

No more let Life divide what Death can join together

And cold hopes swarm like worms within our living clay

  In *Adonais,* from which these examples come, the antithetical style is complemented by many other arresting devices of irony—self-deconstructing personifications, personification in claustrophobic plenitude, catastrophic reversal of conventional patterns of imagery—not to mention what the poem actually says. Contrast and irony permeate representation at every level. The same is true of *The Triumph of Life,* the unending sentences of whose terza rima rhyme scheme lend themselves to waves of shocking antitheses.

          Behind,
Old men, and women foully disarrayed
 Shake their grey hair in the insulting wind,

Limp in the dance and strain with limbs decayed
 To reach the car of light which leaves them still
Farther behind and deeper in the shade.

 But not the less with impotence of will
They wheel, though ghastly shadows interpose
 Round them and round each other, and fulfill

Their work, and to the dust whence they arose
 Sink and corruption veils them as they lie.—
And frost in these performs what fire in those.
           (165–75)

This passage has the power of coherence that cannot be gainsaid: the useless frenzy of the victims, the extremity of the degradation they suffer, and the violent precision of the style are all one. *The Triumph of Life* adheres with remarkable virtuosity to this mode except in one place. The style changes from antithetical to easy and harmonious with the appearance of the seductive "shape all light" who moves to the music of the poem's soft sibilants:

> A shape all light, which with one hand did fling
> Dew on the earth, as if she were the Dawn
> Whose invisible rain forever seemed to sing
>
> A silver music on the mossy lawn
> (352–55)

The nostalgic beauty of this shape and of the style that commemorates her are deceptive, for behind this beauty is still the malevolent deceit of Life. That the shape incarnates this deceit, we discover when Rousseau, returning the poem to its antithetical norm, explains that her movements induce oblivion in anyone who watches her, "As if the gazer's mind was strewn beneath / Her feet like embers, and she, thought by thought / Trampled its fires into the dust of death" (386–88). *The Triumph of Life* in this way consumes a poetic style alternative to the antithetical sublime.

Two earlier poems, "The Song of Apollo" and "The Song of Pan," had already meditated this flourishing of the tragic sense and its partner, the antithetical or severe style. Apollo is the avatar of perspicuous representation in its narrow meaning—as unveiled vision capable of impassive, wide survey. Pan stands at the origin of wisdom literature, authoring tragic generalization. As in the contest of "L'Allegro" and "Il Penseroso," the proponent of tragic vision wins. The exigencies of literary power incline philosophical perspective toward tragic representation. This trauma takes place in the last stanza in the "Song of Pan":

> I sang of the dancing stars,
> I sang of the daedal Earth,
> And of Heaven, and the giant wars,

> And Love and Death and Birth;
>   And then I changed my pipings,
>   Singing how, down the vales of Maenalus
>   I pursued a maiden, and clasped a reed.
>   Gods and men, we are all deluded thus!—
>   It breaks in our bosom and then we bleed;
>   They wept as, I think, both ye now would,
> If envy or age had not frozen your blood,
>   At the sorrow of my sweet pipings.

The antithetical style makes its appearance with the "change" in Pan's pipings. "I pursued a maiden and clasped a reed" is a startling brachiology, almost a zeugma, in the fashion of *Adonais*'s "their father and their prey." For this sharp condensation, Shelley had discarded two mellifluous possibilities, "And sang of Syrinx, the bright maiden / Whom I once loved & could forever," and "Singing of Syrinx, how she became a reed." Shelley was willing to forego the delicious sound of "Syrinx" in order to produce the anonymous formula "a maiden . . . a reed" (Chernaik 238). This revision is absolutely right: the anonymity of the figure and the painful brachiology of the formula contribute to the theme of phantasmal transference and hence strengthen the unexcepting severity of Pan's conclusion, "Gods and men, we are all deluded thus!" That Shelley always revised for sharpness and concision (see the drafts of "Ozymandias"), that this revision is not particular, in no way interferes with its implications. Some of the sorrow of the "Song of Pan" arises out of the attention that it draws to this immanence of sublime rigor. The greater phenomenon is the ascendancy of tragic vision, which manifests itself and enhances its power through the rhetorical superiority of the antithetical style.

The Delusive Flame

Written in the gentler mode associated with the "shape all light," Shelley's late lyrics are all invested with an oddly self-denigrating character: they represent themselves as the remains of an obsolete perspective.[2] Shelley drafted his second-to-last poem, the unfinished "Lines written in the Bay of Lerici" within the manuscript of *The Triumph of Life,* between lines 280 and 281 ("And so my words were seeds of misery / Even as the deeds of others") (Keach 233–34). In spite of being unfinished, "Lines Written in the Bay of Lerici" seems to deal most directly with the emotional crux that the other lyrics either treat by way of evocation ("With a Guitar. To Jane"; "To Jane ('The keen stars were twinkling')") or touch on only in passing as they move toward other conclusions inherent in their governing conceits ("The Invitation," "The Recollection," "The Magnetic Lady to Her Patient"). For Shelley's last lyric takes as its subject the speaker's hopeless relation to his own fantasy and nostalgia. It records its speaker's failed effort not to break the surface of his licensed reverie, reverie that is thin because it cannot not forget what it is and therefore cannot keep at bay the grim thoughts that underlie it. What arrives to disturb the speaker's fragile peace and to set itself against any potential for mild imagination is the tyranny of the antithetical style and the tragic sense.

> Bright wanderer, fair coquette of Heaven,
> To whom alone it has been given
> To change and be adored for ever . . .
> Envy not this dim world, for never
> But once within its shadow grew
> One fair as thou, but far more true.

This is a strange beginning, if these lines do begin the poem.[3] On the one hand, Shelley in typical fashion uses the frame of eulogy to strike a note of disappointment and weariness (compare *Epipsychidion*): he takes the occasion of hymning the moon to recall "this dim world" and its "shadow" and to praise Jane as the one sad exception to the world's sterility. There is a familiar sharpness in some of these lines: the moon is defined by contrast with our world, as the one "to whom alone it has been given" to be loved perpetually; it is exhorted not to envy this inadequate world, for only once did a being of that world rival its beauty. Shelley also makes a surprising choice in the line "for never / But once within its shadow grew"; naturally, we expect growth, particularly of plant life, to take place within or under light, not in shadow. With such phrases,

Shelley adopts the rhetoric of astringent intelligence—that which does not shrink from enunciating the exact, unfriendly truth. The firmness of these unconditional generalizations and negative definitions we recognize from other Shelley poems characterized by their severity. But on the other hand, these lines from "Lerici" simultaneously set themselves free in a kind of unmeaning poetic fancy: the moon is the "fair coquette of Heaven," a "Bright wanderer" competing with mortal women for the honors of beauty. The familiar truth-telling sharpness contrasts with the pastoral conceit of the moon as coquette. Yet in the emotional logic of the poem, unswerving knowledge does not contradict the seemingly alien spirit of idle reverie. In fact, they are complementary; the fantasy is idle because it has been discountenanced in advance.

It is hard to say which stance is uppermost in this passage—melancholy resignation, fierce if disappointed idealism, or fanciful extemporization. Shelley's language has produced some odd union of these attitudes. His tone is that of a constant, disillusioned intelligence, keen and precise, with resources of passion, still, and perfected rhetorical skills it is resigned to bestowing on a limited object. There *is* passion in the dramatic conclusion to the long-suspended opening sentence, which comes to a climax with "One fair as thou, but far more true"; yet this passion has pent itself in a stunted frame. Shelley is serious, but serious in a mode that knows it is trifling. The purpose of this frivolity is only gradually revealed as it becomes more intent:

> She left me at the silent time
> When the moon had ceased to climb
> The azure dome of Heaven's steep,
> And like an albatross asleep,
> Balanced on her wings of light,
> Hovered in the purple night,
> Ere she sought her Ocean nest
> In the chambers of the west.—

This passage establishes the suspended quality of the halcyon moment—this moment after Jane's departure, while the tranquillity she brought lingers on, but only as an opiate tranquillity, shallow and evanescent. This is an anodyne but not a cure. The speaker is permitted, both by this temporary reprieve and by the relaxing of vigilance that comes with his deliberate, dreamy state, to range among distracting images. But these images are timorous and pale, as if his disused power of fantasy had grown infirm. Experience has quelled its energy and taught it its obsolescence. Yet this power of fantasy also remains cautious because the speaker's troubled mind has not really been tranquilized or lulled asleep. He is trying to maintain a delicate balance of wakefulness and peace, consciousness and repose. For this reason, he moves gingerly over the surface of thoughts that promise to be remote and mild; but his tentative search cannot help touching on the reminders of his unhappiness.

The images in this passage are of a becalming nature, as befits the "silent time" they evoke. The moon, at the acme of its ascent, hovers like a bird in the deep-colored night. Its hovering is steady and serene, though not without some suspense (as the notion of "balancing" implies), since it will at any moment turn toward its descent. But it will only be descending toward home, its "Ocean nest," where the "chambers" of sleep lie cradled in the late warmth of the western sky. These childlike, comforting images are the stuff of fairy tales and lullabies, sweet vagaries rising up from an imagination that promises to be and remain benign. Shelley's image of the poised, sleeping albatross and the even more dazzling image it engenders of the moon balancing on "wings of light" stand as figures for the mental balance, the "still time" that the speaker is trying to preserve, in which his mind can expatiate without colliding into the sources of pain; and at the same time, these figures show what sort of soothing, generous imaginings must typify and sustain his frail reprieve.

The next movement of the poem shows the abasement of the speaker's imaginative life:

> She left me, and I staid alone
> Thinking over every tone,
> Which though now silent to the ear
> The enchanted heart could hear
> Like notes which die when born, but still
> Haunt the echoes of the hill:
> And feeling ever—O too much—

> The soft vibrations of her touch
> As if her gentle hand even now
> Lightly trembled o'er my brow;
> And thus although she absent were
> Memory gave me all of her
> That even fancy dares to claim.—

What is it that memory gives him of her? The sound of her voice and the touch of her hand on his brow. It is startling that this is all he would "dare to claim" even in fantasy. In these careful lines, Shelley portrays a fantasy life so chastened and subdued that the rather tame truth can satisfy it. There is a little flourish of chivalry in this—so profound are the consolations of her mere touch—but even this feeble politesse corroborates the sense of the speaker's debilitation. As in "The Magnetic Lady," he is the ailing patient, the subdued, grateful recipient of her magical ministrations. Comforting and reviving powers flow from her voice and her touch, as from those of the Magnetic Lady:

> My hand is on thy brow,
> My spirit on thy brain;
> My pity on thy heart, poor friend;
> And from my fingers flow
> The powers of life, and like a sign,
> Seal thee from thine hour of woe.
>   (*Poetical Works*)

Jane's voice and touch have essentially the same hushing effect in the lines from "Lerici," though Shelley has translated the therapy out of an esoteric or mystical context into a more urbane setting. As a consequence, an air of futility characterizes the interlude that transpires when "she left me, and I staid alone." The speaker does not come away from the rendezvous with his beloved in an exalted or disappointed or hopeful or moved frame of mind. He is like the moon at apogee, listening for the remembered voice and the remembered touch to resonate within him. The "enchanted heart" falls under a marvelous spell. Yet this reverie does not belong to the world of love. The voice and the touch he remembers contained no promises for him; these are futureless caresses, idle, belated, or unanswerable, vanishing in the instant like "notes which die when born." They echo in his mind because they are welcome in the form of echoes; they are what he wants, though they are airy and insubstantial and just barely not the fruit of his own indulged imagination. In its very meagerness, this sustenance satisfies him.

These minimally stirring memories introduce the more familiar pathos in the alienation of the deaf ear and the enchanted heart—that is to say, in the separation of the two worlds: the barren, real one and the imaginative one that compensates it. In the former, absent voices have no sound; but in the world of wish fulfillment, imagination restores presence and pleasure in lingering reflections—reflections that soothe, however empty they are known to be. The imagined world hovers over the true one. Shelley, however, has added a characteristic twist here, turning the tenor out of sync with the vehicle to perturbing effect. The sound of Jane's voice resonates in memory the way that notes reappear in their afterechoes; but when the echo is internalized, it must lose its real sound, reduced to dead silence again for all but the speaker, with his "enchanted heart." Unlike an echo, the memory of a sound is not a sound. An idealized memory of a sound is the dream remaining to this demoralized speaker.

It ought to be clear by now that this is not a love poem. Some later lines make this vivid:

> Her presence had made weak and tame
> All passions, and I lived alone,
> In the time which is our own.

Though it is certainly a curious thing to say of your beloved that her presence has left your passions "weak and tame," this line does not come as a surprise; it follows from the spirit of the rest of the poem in which stillness seems to provide the most suitable answer to the speaker's diminished desires. In fact, the line essentially summarizes the implications of the previous passage, which pictures the speaker suspended in reverie, carefully prolonging his superficial calm through the memory of Jane's assuaging presence (she has done him the good he says insofar as she has tamed "*All* passions"). The arresting line is the one that follows: "and I lived alone / In the time which is our own." This phrase has the form of an affirmation, but its meaning is a little dark, for the moment it describes is one of abatement, isolation, and exclusion; it gives the freedom of a kind of void. As the next lines explain, "The past and future were forgot / As they had been and would be, not." The time is "our own" in the sense of being the singular present, free from remorse and nostalgia as well as from the stirring emotions related to futurity—hope, "Desire & Fear."

The speaker has hushed himself in a willing silence. As the image of the balancing moon offers an image for the exempted moment that the poem describes, so the image of the hill with its echoes "haunted" by delicate, dying notes figures something in the speaker's emotional condition—his frailty, passivity, and wishfully absent stance—as well as the defensive strategy by which he attempts to preserve this brittle peace as he fixes on the distracting thoughts suitable to his chastened imagination. This pattern of subdued echoing figures also the modus operandi of the poem, which captures the inclinations of the speaker with its lulling rhythms, its fragile pastoral atmosphere, and its drifting course of innocuous images. What is strange about these figures—the balanced moon, the haunted echoes—is that, as figures for the speaker's condition or the poem's structure, they already overlap so intimately with what they describe. The speaker's pause of tranquillity is not only like the pause of the moon at apogee; it takes place under the auspices of that moment. The haunted echoes not only suggest the method of the speaker's distraction; they appear as a metaphor for an instance of that kind of distraction. The central images of the poem thus do a kind of double duty, serving as both metaphor and metonymy. Their overdetermination testifies to the imaginative fixation that is the subject of the poem. The same ideas keep returning with a lulling circularity.

The lines that follow set the tranquil moment off by interrupting it. The syncope of indifference crumbles with the words "But soon": "But soon the guardian angel gone, the demon reassumed his throne / In my faint heart." This is the first interruption of the speaker's pursuit after the peace of a gracious imagination; naturally it is the demon of his own thoughts, from which he has sought to drift, that now ensnares him. Just as I have reverted to a lurid vocabulary in using the words "ensnares" and "dreaded," so Shelley reverts here to melodramatic language—to language more highly charged than ever, with its vaguely fabulous allusions to demons and kings. His melodramatic phrases create intensity in the moment, but they also mimic the exaggerated, harassing character of the images produced by that newly awakened, ghastly imagination, instigator of thoughts he "dare not speak." Under their pressure, the speaker for the first time openly characterizes himself as debilitated; the demon takes the throne in his "faint heart," and thus he finds himself sitting in silence, aghast, "disturbed and weak." The implication seems to be that the reemergence of the demon has shaken him, rendering the heart faint in which the demon finds sovereignty, but also that his disappointments have enfeebled him permanently.

The interference of the demon prefaces the subtler but more definitive interruption of the fisher with his "delusive flame"; his appearance signals the acknowledged failure and the end of therapeutic imaginings. But for the moment the speaker succeeds in retracing his way to the kindness of fantasy, indeed to the most wishful, elaborate, and implicitly ill-fated of his reveries:

> But soon, the guardian angel gone,
> The demon reassumed his throne
> In my faint heart . . . I dare not speak
> My thoughts; but thus disturbed and weak
> I sate and watched the vessels glide
> Along the ocean bright and wide,
> Like spirit-winged chariots sent
> O'er some serenest element
> To ministrations strange and far;
> As if to some Elysian star
> They sailed for drink to medicine
> Such sweet and bitter pain as mine.

In the ellipsis points there is a pause, an evasion and a recovery that turns out to be less than full. Elizabeth Bishop makes the same psychologically telling use of ellipsis points in her poem "At the Fishouses"; in the final stanza, the speaker dodges the thought that knowledge, heavy, grim, and hard to gain, is also impermanent. She begins to formulate this thought but then stops short, diverting herself and digressing into a kind of fancy that, wistful and wry, betrays her consciousness of its inefficacy:

> Cold dark deep and absolutely clear,
> element bearable to no mortal,
> to fish and to seals . . . One seal particularly
> I have seen here evening after evening.
> He was curious about me. He was interested in music;
> like me a believer in total immersion,
> so I used to sing him Baptist hymns.
> I also sang "A Mighty Fortress Is Our God."
> He stood up in the water and regarded me
> steadily, moving his head a little.
> Then he would disappear, then suddenly emerge
> almost in the same spot, with a sort of shrug
> as if it were against his better judgment.

The next line resumes with the unwelcome refrain "Cold dark deep and absolutely clear." In the ellipsis points, the speaker has knowingly regressed from the thought she does not want to think to a good-natured fantasy. Now she lets herself imagine in a credulous fashion that animals are like people and want to communicate with us. In her fantasy, she renders the world benevolent. But her vagaries are touched with self-conscious irony ("He was interested in music; / like me a believer in total immersion"), ironies meant to indicate that she knows she is indulging herself. Yet her sadness at this knowledge and her wish that what she is wishing could be true come through in a moment of projection not well enough ironized: "He stood up in the water and regarded me / steadily, moving his head a little." Like hers, Shelley's fantasy is internally compromised, a bubble of the thinnest texture. What sustains it is not enjoyment or forgetfulness but reluctance and delay and the knowledge of its emptiness. It is a bad-faith fantasy, permeated by the speaker's self-consciousness and regret. It is elaborated in proportion as it is disbelieved.

The speaker turns away from his thoughts to look at the ocean, where ships "gliding" calmly over the beautiful waters, "bright and wide," contrast with his own state. In their silent, seemingly peaceful absorption, the ships give him the matter for dreaming on. He sees them as plying their way on a mission of mercy, transformed out of mundanity into "chariots" with the wings of spirits, sailing over a sea elevated into "some serenest element." This is a sufficiently fabulous fantasy, but now the speaker adds that they are sailing away to extravagant "ministrations," "strange and far," "as if"—here the dream gets wilder—they sailed to "some Elysian star," to find a supernatural pharmacon for his impossible illness. Shelley sustains to breathlessness the long sentence in which this idyll is elaborated; he grants the fantasy a kind of syntactical reprieve, a space for the idly marvelous to bloom; but the words with which the sentence finally ends also bring to an end this billowing fiction, when the oppression that lay behind it and propelled it resurges. In fact, the speaker has never escaped and forgotten; the extravagance of his reverie was prompted, and excused, by the clarity of his consciousness. He is dreaming falsely, as alert as he can be, and the frail surface of the bubble, his alienated reverie, breaks at the touch: "As if to some Elysian star / They sailed for drink to medicine / Such sweet and bitter pain as mine." With the words "Such sweet and bitter pain," the speaker quietly reinstates the dark certainty that has never left him. The off-rhyme of "medicine" and "mine" serves to sound the note of returning gravity, as Shelley's off-rhymes often do. The truth returns, gently but inevitably, because it has never been far away. And thus the speaker takes the tone not of complaint but of acknowledgment: he is detailing the truth with that clarity and oddly impersonal sadness we have already seen. Even the pairing of "sweet and bitter" echoes the language of the lost reverie, the "ministrations strange and far."

The mention of this pain informs us of the speaker's continuing objectivity, but it does so lightly, without any irreversible violence, so that it is possible for happy and lulling thoughts to resume with the following lines.

> And the wind that winged their flight
> From the land came fresh and light,
> And the scent of sleeping flowers
> And the coolness of the hours
> Of dew, and the sweet warmth of day
> Was scattered o'er the twinkling bay.

Here the echoes of lullaby and fairy tale are stronger than ever. A soothing parataxis rocks the lines; an enchanting synesthesia evokes the hushed, magical atmosphere of evening. Shelley may not have read Blake's "To the Evening Star," but these lines are very like it; they too describe the twilight as liberal, suspending and reversing the order of the world, so that it is briefly hospitable to delicate and vulnerable things. Everything promises benignity; the wind wings the flight of the healing angels, the flowers emit sweet scent, the day is obliging and warm, the dew is refreshing and cool, the waters of the bay twinkle invitingly, like the lights of the awakening stars. As in fairy tales, a dim anthropomorphism permits the natural world to take on these appearances of benevolence and of fragility. The wind that arrives "fresh and light," the warmth of the day, called "sweet," and even the waters that "twinkle" and smile have all assumed, however faintly, the tenderness of mortal agents. The flowers that sleep in the elegant wind, exhaling their lovely "scent" like baby's breath, recall the more stirring anthropomorphism of Blake's poem: "Scatter thy silver dew / On every flower that shuts its sweet eyes / In timely sleep." In Shelley's evocation of the liminal twilight, as in Blake's, wishes worthy of childhood are expressed in the fictions of childhood. In the modesty of the scene and in the kindness and vulnerability of its creatures the speaker has rendered the idealized version of his desolate inner life. He has transferred his fatalism to the scene in the form of its pastoral tameness; he has substituted regression for his fatigue.

The author of this wishfulness has agreed to indulge his capacity for fantasy as if blind to it, or rather, as if to restrain it had become superfluous, because he has already given up on it. That is what the following lines suggest, for the end of his digressive project comes as no surprise. The lines that bring on this end are continuous with the ones that come before them; they seem to keep up the placid elaboration of the twilight's magic. "And the fisher with his lamp and spear." A human figure, apparently a pastoral figure, enters the scene; he is viewed at a distance, plying his trade in quiet, like the "spirit-winged" ships. That he carries a "spear" seems a little ominous, but it is actually the metrical quality of the following words that begins to entangle and damage the pastoral fantasy. The lines lose their lulling anapestic-iambic rhythm with the cramped consonants, the spondee, and the dramatic trochee in "about the low rocks damp / Crept and. . . ." That the next word should be "struck" seems almost to be predicted from the disturbance of the rhythm.

What the fisher "strikes" are avatars of the speaker and his wishfulness, "the fish who came / To worship the delusive flame." The "delusive flame" is the ignis fatuus, or will-o'-the-wisp, a common image of uncanniness and treachery. But Shelley has added the disturbing thought of acute mystification, of "worshipping" the delusive light. His description is both sympathetic and satirical. The pious fish, somewhat stupid, somewhat innocent, are brutally deceived; they are caught out in the pursuit of something wonderful, the "flame" burning on the shore, the mirage of an ideal that has too late revealed its emptiness. This picture contains the irony and regret of an autobiographical reflection. Thus, despite what is for us the startling density of this antithesis, "the delusive flame," it comes easily to the speaker. There is no pause for him to see that the flame is delusive; no discovery is entailed. He knew it all along, and he is now surrendering his futile effort to postpone the recognition. He cannot turn his uncomforting mind from its trained purposes. He gives up with the succeeding lines, which radically change the style of discourse, forsaking the lyrical, imaginative mode for a strict and severe generalization. The sternness of the aphorism takes over, and however we may choose to interpret these unfinished lines, their genre guarantees that they be harsh, summary, and impersonal. The lines were in flux when Shelley abandoned them, and it seems impossible now to give them any exact meaning; but it is clear at least that they characterize the fishes' fate as desirable, in so far as their pleasure, once attained, brings "extinction" of "the sense and thought" of regret—of such useless regret as the speaker entertains in his vigil. The speaker's liberal imaginings fail, and he reverts to the stony truths he is inured to. Yet the change is not climactic: the speaker merely ceases to contend with what he has had to acknowledge from the beginning, that one cannot regress at will.

The poem contains movement and suspense; despite its quest for stillness, it is dramatic. Yet the speaker ends where he began, and everything remains as it is. The poem is impacted and introverted: there are no lines out at all, not even spurious ones like that taken by Byron in "On This Day I Complete My Thirty-Sixth Year." "Lerici's" movements take the form of very slight, very subtle zigzaggings within a narrow track, for they represent the motions of a mind with not much of any place to go. The psychological state adumbrated here consists of disappointment, not so much with the world and its opportunities as with a particular life that appears to have exhausted its possibilities prematurely. This state of disappointment does not strike the sufferer as an intellectually interesting condition. It is personal and contingent and therefore not stimulating to discourse or analysis in the way that a more general disillusionment, with some greater objects, might be. For the consequence of such disappointment is precisely to reveal to the subject that, however pressing his unease is to him, it has no weight, uniqueness, or general importance. If we take Stevens's "desire without an object of desire" to describe the quandary of disillusionment with all potential libidinal investments, then this is not quite the speaker's predicament, since in his case it is not external objects but his own existence that he regards with distrust and disdain. Because it is his particular life that has somehow failed, he finds himself in a quandary as to how he may occupy his unextinguishable, if curtailed, resources of imagination and desire. What he wishes is to wish, but his wishes are discredited before he can indulge them. The speaker's imaginative and libidinal energies are driven backward into nostalgia and reverie of an especially fragile and specious order. This acute self-limitation gives rise to the poem's introversion and circularity.

The poem represents its own lyricism as an indulgence and an anachronism. This is the dark side of its status as a suspended time. What brings it up short, what represents the intrusion of the reality principle, is the antithetical style: "my faint heart," "such sweet and bitter pain," "the delusive flame." Most of Shelley's late lyrics, including "To Jane," "With a Guitar. To Jane," "The Serpent Is Shut Out from Paradise," and, as we have seen, "The Recollection," share this poem's inobtrusive rhymes and diction, its mood of tamed reverie, and its knowledge of its own status as fantasy. But "Lerici" makes it clear that an opposing style, with its opposing definition of intelligence and literary power, has routed the hope of the lyric. There is a kind of division in Shelley's own mind between his affective interests and the tendency of his literary skills. The innovations of his antitragic lyricism had continued to exercise his literary talent in their own way, but when this lyricism was separated from its aesthetic and political agenda, it became the lively or gentle or urbane poetics of these late poems, which by virtue of their self-denial come to lend themselves to the tragic sense.

Shelley's Arc

It may seem as if over the course of his life, Shelley followed an itinerary in which each phase of his thought exposed the comparative naïveté of the previous phase and accelerated by one order of magnitude in the sublimity of its darkness. But, as we have seen, the self-transumptions of skepticism already shape the rhetorical structure of his individual poems. In addition, Shelley's poetry already—and repeatedly—dramatizes the incorporation of debilitating insight into the truth—from *Alastor* to *Julian and Maddalo* to *The Triumph of Life*. His own interest in this theme has paradoxically given rise to odd superstitions about the prophetic nature of his poetry. It is not uncommon for critics to describe *Alastor* as the prophecy of Shelley's own fate. Indeed, in "The Zucca," a poem of 1822, the scenario of "Lift Not the Painted Veil" befalls the first person:

> I loved—oh, no, I mean not one of ye,
>   Or any earthly one, though ye are dear
> As human heart to human heart may be;—
>   I loved, I know not what—but this low sphere
> And all that it contains, contains not thee
>   (*Poetical Works*)

What prevents us from calling "Lift Not the Painted Veil" a "prophecy" of Shelley's eventual disillusionment, as detailed in "The Zucca," is the very fact that Shelley had written "Lift Not the Painted Veil." That he began in a preoccupation with the itinerary of tragic discovery makes it difficult to persist in describing the course of his career as a blind enactment of it. He had a literarily-inspired interest in the nature of tragic knowledge. But, as the peculiar rhetorical structure of "Lift Not the Painted Veil" suggests, the changes in Shelley's poetry itself do not represent the movement from blessed ignorance to tragic knowledge. A more subtle movement within knowledge was in fact the subject of a curious fragment from 1820:

> Alas! this is not what I thought life was.
> I knew that there were crimes and evil men,
> Misery and hate; nor did I hope to pass
> Untouched by suffering, through the rugged glen,
> In mine own heart I saw as in a glass
> The hearts of others   And when
> I went among my kind, with triple brass
> Of calm endurance my weak breast I armed,
> To bear scorn, fear, and hate, a woful mass!
>   (*Poetical Works* 633–34)

The fragment breaks off just at the point of distinguishing the speaker's preexperiential knowledge from his experiential discoveries, though it takes work to imagine what dark truth he had yet to learn. The distinction may have been difficult to tease out as a constative one, a difference in the content of knowledge. As long as dark generalization has to go in search of its content, then its increasing success cannot properly be ascribed to the result of deepening knowledge. The temptation is to portray the difference between early and late Shelley as a difference in ideas, but the difference—sometimes in ideas, sometimes in style, intensity, or expertise—actually reflects a constant progress along a route determined by an autonomous literary imperative. The severity of truth lost its literariness for Shelley at the same time that he was becoming more literarily expert at it, perhaps because he *was* becoming more expert, and his regret sunk through the levels to transparency. The tenuousness of its difference remained for literature but failed for Shelley, in the manner of the scattered reflections in the pool of purple light.

The odd sense of circularity or tautology in Shelley's career—the way in which his poetry seems to have predicted its own fate as well as Shelley's fate and to have accomplished a trajectory toward tragedy with which it was always pregnant—reflects its obedience to a necessity within literature. Shelley ends with the strong sense of fate in *Adonais* and *The*

Triumph of Life because in one phase of this cycle, not perhaps the last, poetry takes as its subject a necessity that it represents under a different name, such as "life," but that is in fact a necessity proper to literature itself. In Aeschylus this necessity is given the name Fate, and it is part of a religion; the impersonality of Aeschylean poetics attempts to convey its nature and resonance, as does, in turn, the severity of style in Weil and Johnson. In Shelley's work there is some confusion between the "fate" of his poetics and that of his person. Everyone who studies Shelley senses the force of necessity that propels his poetry toward its seemingly natural and inevitable end. But those who write about this force rationalize it by representing its bending arc as the emanation of Shelley's gradual and unforeseen disillusionment. Thus, while Judith Chernaik may write that "these last lyrics confirm the darkening of [Shelley's] spirit," his "pessimism," and the "withdrawal" of his hopes (177), or while Bloom may praise "the wisdom of disillusion" that Shelley achieved after *Epipsychidion* and the "realistic sorrow and wisdom" to which he ascended in *The Triumph of Life* (*Visionary Company* 335), they are only giving naturalizing and spiritualizing names to a literary necessity to which they respond at the same time in thinking, as they manifestly do, that Shelley's "disillusionment" and "darkening" were the best and brightest fulfillment of the dream of his poems. The themes of demystification and dawning undelight themselves take shape within the paradigm of the truth's grimness. Shelley's critics follow this paradigm in perceiving his mind to have darkened, and in this way they echo the vocation of his poetry.

Paul de Man's seminal essay "Shelley Disfigured" has the distinction of questioning this picture of Shelley's deepening knowledge. But it finds other means by which to participate in the paradigm of the grimness of the truth. Oddly, the essay that attributes to the poem an exact and accurate apprehension of the "linguistic predicament" that de Man himself studied to uncover. Its "negative knowledge" does not of course prevent the poem from suffering the random textual articulation it describes, since it is fractured by "the actual death and subsequent disfigurement of Shelley's body" (120). But de Man does not argue, as he does in roughly contemporaneous essays on Wordsworth and Rousseau, that the text itself regresses from its knowledge. "The Triumph of Life" perfected an austerity that de Man recapitulates, changing the vocabulary but not the resonance of the poem's skeptical fierceness. In "The Triumph of Life," de Man's writing found a comparable text to enlist in its own enterprise of consolidating philosophical precision and rhetorical severity. Given de Man's fascination with intellectual asceticism, it is perhaps not surprising that even his rhetorical analysis, "Shelley Disfigured," should reproduce a description of Shelley's career in which Shelley's last poem—if not Shelley himself—should perform a "rigorous" demystification of all his earlier work.

Shelley and his friends imagined that he had fulfilled the destiny of literature at his own expense. The necessity on which his work was bent seemed to rob his material life of its autonomy, producing a sense that he was ethereal and that his existence was spurious. (We recall that Weil described a similar attenuation of her personality.) When shortly after Shelley's death Mary Shelley wrote, "All say that he was an elemental spirit imprisoned here but free & happy now" (*Letters* 178), she echoed the lines from "With a Guitar. To Jane" in which Shelley lamented the incarnation of Ariel: "And now, alas, the poor sprite is / Imprisoned for some fault of his / In a body like a grave." He had written similarly to Claire Clairemont, "I can do you no other good than in keeping up the unnatural connexion between this feeble mass of diseases and infirmities and the vapid & weary spirit doomed to drag it through the world" (*Letters* 2:257). His life appeared to have separated out from life. It confirms this impression that in the margin beside the last lines of "The Triumph of Life," Shelley wrote in a small hand, "Alas, I kiss you, Jane" (Holmes 724). Conversely, the immanence and impersonal authority of tragic representation make themselves manifest when stern, anonymous scriptural prophecies begin to float over the pages of his last notebook: "Thou shalt be hidden from the scourge of the angel—thou shalt be in league with the stones of the field"; "Thou makest me to possess the iniquities of my youth" (Holmes 726). These harsh words are as ominous as the intrusion of "the delusive flame" into the dream-world of "Lerici."

In her note on the poems of 1822, Mary Shelley ascribes to Shelley's poetry a strange collusion with his death (an ascription that many others make, including some contemporary critics):

Though dreams and hues of poetry cannot blunt grief, it invests his fate with a sublime fitness, which those less nearly allied may regard with complacency. A year before he had poured into verse all such ideas about death as give it a glory of its own. He had, as it now seems, almost anticipated his own destiny; and when the mind figures his skiff wrapped from sight by the thunder-storm, as it was last seen upon the purple sea, and then, as the cloud of the tempest passed away, no sign remained of where it had been—who but will regard as a prophecy the last stanza of the *Adonais?* (*Poetical Works* 679)

Despite the frisson of uncanniness lingering about these quotations, it is not the case that literature conspired in Shelley's death but that the specter of this uncanny possibility arose when his life conformed to the fateful arc pursued by his poetry. The "sublime fitness" of which Mary Shelley wrote, the conformation of Shelley's life to the designs of his poetry, is a variant of the "sublime fitness" occasioned by the successful self-transumption of tragic skepticism. Shelley's poetry recreated the grimness of the truth, and his life illustrates its meaning.

CHAPTER 6

Wittgenstein's Melancholy

In my introduction, I described some of Wittgenstein's strategies for isolating what is paradigmatic in the tragic sense and dispelling its spurious authority. During the time that Wittgenstein was developing his later philosophy, he evidently wanted to question the prestige of the tragic paradigm, indeed to defy it, by placing it among the "captivating pictures" and "misrepresentations" of "our language." These "captivating pictures" include many of the subjects of traditional philosophy; and Wittgenstein might have grouped the tragic sense together with them insofar as they all are or could be, in his view, diseases of analytical enterprise. It was a certain fatalistic element in psychoanalysis, with its "tragic scenarios" of predetermined behavior, that gave Wittgenstein pause and made him launch his critique. But he was also fascinated and moved by Freud. And there is good reason to think he was uneasy about the seductions of fatalism and sadness precisely because he recognized their hold on him. For in spite of his effort to undermine and elude the attractions of the tragic sense, he could not fully relinquish it in his own writing, particularly in his major late work, *Philosophical Investigations*. For a writer of his literary aspiration—acknowledged or not—to surrender pathos would have been to surrender a major source of power and conviction. Wittgenstein's later philosophy provides the terms for understanding the archaic and deep-rooted fascinations of the tragic paradigm. But the tenacity of the paradigm is such that Wittgenstein himself was not able to escape it.

Chapter 6

The Bewitchment of Language

"What looks as if it *had* to exist, is part of the language" (no. 50): this is Wittgenstein's classic expression of mistrust toward the paradigm of essentiality.[1] Because he suspected the appearance of the inexorable, Wittgenstein wished to describe language without invoking metaphysical necessity. He could not grant a force of inevitable necessity even to the workings of language, so in 1930, repudiating his claim in the *Tractatus* that "the limits of my language are the limits of my world" and that "what we cannot speak about we must pass over in silence," he corrected himself: "Thrusting against the limits of language? Language is not a cage" ("Lecture on Ethics" 16). In the *Investigations* he sought to repicture language as intertwined with human behavior in more subtle forms than his earlier metaphors of confinement and limitation had suggested.

This antideterminism lies behind his insistence on the "game" in "language-games" and the rejection of synthesis in the term "family resemblances." "Language" as such does not exist; there are instead language-games that belong to a diverse set of activities. To the extent that paraphrases of Wittgenstein involve hypostatizing the categories of "language," "people," and the like, they betray him in his ambition to escape from essentialism and determinism, as he firmly expressed it early on in the *Investigations*.

> Here the term "language-*game*" is meant to bring into prominence the fact that the *speaking* of language is part of an activity or of a form of life.
>
> Review the multiplicity of language-games in the following examples, and in others:
>
> Giving orders, and obeying them—
> Describing the appearance of an object, or giving its measurements—
> Constructing an object from a description (a drawing)—
> Reporting an event—
> Speculating about an event—
> Forming and testing an hypothesis—
> Presenting the results of an experiment in tables and diagrams—

Making up a story; and reading it—
Play-acting—
Singing catches—
Guessing riddles—
Making a joke; telling it—
Solving a problem in practical arithmetic—
Translating from one language into another—
Asking, thanking, cursing, greeting, praying.

—It is interesting to compare the multiplicity of the tools in language and of the ways they are used, the multiplicity of kinds of word and sentence, with what logicians have said about the structure of language. (Including the author of the *Tractatus Logico-Philosophicus*). (no. 23)

The absorption of language may be deep, but its work is all there on the surface. Thus Wittgenstein's project will not be to discover anything occult, unknown, or deeply hidden: "It is . . . of the essence of our investigation that we do not seek to learn anything *new* by it. We want to *understand* something that is already in plain view. For *this* is what we seem in some sense not to understand" (no. 89); "We must do away with all *explanation*, and description alone must take its place. And this description gets its light, that is to say its purpose, from the philosophical problems. These are, of course, not empirical problems; they are solved, rather, by looking into the workings of our language, and that in such a way as to make us recognize those workings; *in despite of* an urge to misunderstand them. The problems are solved, not by giving new information, but by arranging what we have always known" (no. 109). But this refusal to invest language with compulsory and fatalistic powers is not uncomplicated, nor should it be confused with a complacent pragmatism. *Philosophical Investigations* is itself, after all, a powerfully demystifying and delicately sad book, though it comes by its sadness without appealing explicitly to the tragic paradigm.

In Wittgenstein's view, traditional philosophy, by contrast with *his* method, creates a sense of profundity by occulting the implications of its own language. The workings of language can produce the appearance of depth and truth. Wittgenstein warned against such tricks under the name of "bewitchment"—the means by which language leads us unknowingly astray as we trail after those will-o'-the-wisps, "grammatical illusions." It is precisely when philosophy falls prey to these illusions that it seems most serious and powerful—powerful because it unknowingly recapitulates the assumptions of our grammar. ("Grammar" in Wittgenstein means not the system of rules for generating sentences in a specific language but the range of language-games in which a given word is used.) The metaphysical consideration of "thought," for instance, springs from the enchantments of grammar: "'Language (or thought) is something unique'—this proves to be a superstition (*not* a mistake!) itself produced by grammatical illusions" (no. 110). In this analysis, the grammar of the concept of "thought" suggests to us that thought is unique, and we fail to recognize that the grammar is dictating the metaphysical definition of "thought." "Thought" is not in fact a unified phenomenon; we use the word in many different contexts, to describe many different kinds of experience and behavior. And whatever Descartes liked to imagine, thought is even less a mysterious, unique attribute of the mind that separates it forever from the sense-trapped body. "Subliming the logic of our language" is what Wittgenstein calls this confusion of grammar with essence. The notion of subliming brings us back to the idea that logic itself exerts the attraction of "something sublime" and thus introduces the suspicion that what strikes us as deep, profound, or—to use the opposite metaphor—transcendental and exalted derives this appearance from conjuring with the worlds built by grammar.

Philosophical problems, such as the problem of the nature of thought, seem profound when they reiterate the metaphysics idly suggested by our language, because what is suggested by our language strikes us as ineluctable. As Wittgenstein puts it: "The problems arising through a misrepresentation of our forms of language have the character of *depth*. They are deep disquietudes; their roots are as deep in us as the forms of our language and their significance is as great as the importance of our language.—Let us ask ourselves: why do we feel a grammatical joke to be *deep*? (And that is what the depth of philosophy is.)" (no. 111). Philosophical problems and their comic double, the grammatical joke, resonate profoundly because they evoke the ghostly precedents in our language.

One example of a grammatical joke appears in this sentence: "It can't be said of me at all (except perhaps as a joke) that I *know* I am in pain" (no. 246). This claim to knowledge—"I know I am in pain"—tingles with profound wit, not because (as it tantalizingly suggests) it reveals something of the nature of knowledge or of pain or of the self, but because it plays upon the grammar of the concept of knowledge. In *our* concept of knowledge, knowledge is a kind of mental state that involves reasoning, finding out, detecting, learning, and so on—forms of estranged reflection that do not apply to the experience of our own sensations. With an exciting challenge to expectation, the sentence violates the grammar that it invokes in its formation, but with the odd result that it can therefore seem suggestive and serious—if we fail to see through its metaphysical pretensions to its absurdity.

Metaphysics can be found to derive its "insights" from grammatical jokes that it is unaware of making:

> I can know what someone else is thinking, not what I am thinking.
> It is correct to say "I know what you are thinking," and wrong to say "I know what I am thinking."
> (A whole cloud of philosophy condensed into a drop of grammar.)
> (p. 222)

Our concept of "knowledge" also already excludes "knowing" one's own thoughts (as if observing them from outside); thus the grammatical originality of the expression "I know what I am thinking" recommends it to us—spuriously—as a profound reflection. These paragraphs on the concept of knowledge appear in the midst of an investigation that reveals the fallacy of the concept. That concept was always misleading, since it suggests that knowledge is an internal state, whereas knowledge is in fact not like a feeling or a state of consciousness; knowledge does not "occupy the mind" but has its bearing on the public sphere, in action and behavior.

The illusion of metaphysical depth is produced by the fundamentality of the grammatical conventions placed at risk. To hit upon these grammatical foundations creates a vertiginous sense of depth precisely because there is nowhere else to go: as Wittgenstein says in a different context, "I have reached bedrock, and my spade is turned" (no. 217). It is little wonder that so profound a convention, so "deep in us," should exert such a powerful attraction: "A *picture* held us captive. And we could not get outside it, for it lay in our language and language seemed to repeat it to us inexorably" (no. 115).

Though Wittgenstein denies profundity to metaphysical speculation, he clearly does not do away with the metaphor of depth. "Grammatical illusions" *are* profound insofar as we have profoundly absorbed them; they gain their appearance of depth, in other words, from the depth of their significance to our life. Wittgenstein turns to strange and dramatic phrasing in these passages when he says that the forms of our language have some shadowy, tremendous "importance," with "roots" that are "deep in us." This phrasing suggests an unusual image of depth, a paradoxical image of incorporating the surface. According to *Philosophical Investigations,* our acquaintance with language itself proves archaically and almost irretrievably profound: our knowledge of language, as well as the knowledge and the certainties that spring from language-games—both of them more fundamental than the "knowledge" defined by our concepts—result from an absorption that took place long ago, long before we came to ask questions of this continent "deep in us." The depth of language's absorption explains why it is Wittgenstein's task, as he says (and here his discipleship to Freud may be perceived), to "remind" us of something we already know:

> Augustine says in the *Confessions* "quid est ergo tempus? si nemo ex me quaerat scio; si quaerenti explicare velim, nescio."—This could not be said about a question of natural science ("What is the specific gravity of hydrogen?" for instance). Something that we know when no one asks us, but no longer know when we are supposed to give an account of it, is something that we need to *remind* ourselves of. (And it is obviously something of which for some reason it is difficult to remind oneself) (no. 89).

On Certainty is devoted to analyzing this peculiar form of knowledge—which is deep, fundamental, forgotten, inexperienced, and unfelt. Indeed, our experience of "experience" hangs on prior, deeper, so-to-speak anexperiential acquaintance with language-games: "A child can use the names of people long before he can say in any form whatever: 'I know this one's name; I don't know that one's yet'" (no. 543). The sorting of the world follows patterns established by language-games well before specific ostensive definitions, or "naming," can take much hold. Or, to cite a more suggestively radical claim: in part two of the *Investigations*, Wittgenstein says of "aspect-seeing," "The substratum of this experience is the mastery of a technique" (p. 208). In this instance, experience does not arise from the unmediated responsiveness of the subject, but rather, the conditions for the experience are created by acquaintance with language-games. Similarly, because empirical knowledge belongs to the playing of language-games and not to the inner life, "An inner experience cannot shew me that I *know* something" (*On Certainty* no. 569). The systems of belief and knowledge with which language-games are intertwined organize experience at the same time that they are so archaic in us, and so fundamental, that they do not rise to the level of the inner life.

The prime target of *On Certainty* is metaphysical skepticism, which, unaware of our constitutive and conclusive acquaintance with language-games, reverts to doubts that would stand apart and, in a sense, predate them. By treating the inner life as primary and experience as unmediated, metaphysical skepticism makes it possible to doubt the existence of the external world and of other minds (though not of one's own mind). It asks us to doubt what the language in which we would express our doubt prohibits us from meaningfully doubting; as Wittgenstein writes, "My life shews that I know or am certain that there is a chair over there, or a door, and so on" (no. 7). The words that we use commit us to certain beliefs, especially about the existence of the external world and of other minds, and including the intractable belief that the words themselves have meaning. Doubting, on the other hand, merely succeeds and plays upon that archaic, unreasoned, and unjustified form of belief that springs to life with the entry into language-games: "The child learns by believing the adult. Doubt comes *after* belief" (no. 160). It is then impossible for users of language to revert to the stage before belief. But, though this impossibility of meaningfully questioning its subjects makes a chimera of metaphysical skepticism, Wittgenstein does not suggest that his own arguments dispel uncertainty: we can only say that "the *truth* of certain empirical propositions belongs to our frame of reference" (no. 83), or "if you are not certain of any fact, you cannot be certain of the meaning of your words either" (no. 114). The ineluctable origin of our deepest, unspoken certainties does not guarantee that they are grounded in common sense. On the contrary, because the knowledge of language-games begins so early and runs so deep, "the difficulty is to realize the groundlessness of our believing" (no. 166).

"The child learns by believing the adult." The lessons and imitations of childhood form the central interest of *Philosophical Investigations,* whose view of language begins to develop itself in an account of language acquisition. *Philosophical Investigations* deliberately opens with a quotation about Augustine's childhood, but not merely to establish and then dismantle Augustine's primitive confidence in the essentiality of ostensive definition. As Stanley Cavell has maintained, it begins with this quotation in order to introduce the resonant image of the imitating child—and, without Augustine's intending it, the child imitating everything—expressions, movements, states of mind, desires—not just words:

> When they (my elders) named some object, and accordingly moved towards something, I saw this and I grasped that the thing was called by the sound they uttered when they meant to point it out. Their intention was shewn by their bodily movements, as it were the natural language of all peoples: the expression of the face, the play of the eyes, the movement of other parts of the body, and the tone of voice which expresses our state of mind in seeking, having, rejecting, or avoiding something. Thus, as I heard words repeatedly used in their proper places in various sentences, I gradually learnt to understand what objects they signified; and after I had trained my mouth to form these signs, I used them to express my own desires. (no. 1)

We can gain insight into Wittgenstein's argument by reading this paragraph, as it were, literally—bodily movements precede intention; the play of the eyes precedes the state of mind; use precedes signification. It *should* be eerie and disorienting (in the way that *Philosophical Investigations* is) to read, "After I trained my mouth to form these signs, I used them to express my own desires." The phenomena of interiority that would seem to have priority actually develop in tandem with "training" and imitation. Wittgenstein criticizes Augustine most sharply for not treating the child's imitations as original, or radically generative, enough:

> Someone coming into a strange country will sometimes learn the language of the inhabitants from ostensive definitions that they give him; and he will often have to *guess* the meaning of these definitions; and will guess sometimes right, sometimes wrong.
>
> And now, I think, we can say: Augustine describes the learning of human language as if the child came into a strange country and did not understand the language of the country; that is, as if it already had a language, only not this one. Or again: as if the child could already *think*, only not yet speak. And "think" would here mean something like "talk to itself." (no. 32)

The child does not already know the paradigm of what it is imitating (it will learn the paradigm by way of this imitation); it imitates blindly—as an aphorism later in *Philosophical Investigations* says, "I obey the rule *blindly*" (no. 219).

In Wittgenstein's thinking incorporation is primordial—one would like to say prepsychological, since the incorporation of language precedes and enables the development of psychological concepts, or "pictures" of interiority. But the psychoanalytic terminology of "incorporation" is perhaps already too pictorial, too bodily, for this idea. It seems almost impossible not to use physical metaphors in describing Wittgenstein's adumbrations of "incorporation," but this is just what should be avoided. Because Wittgenstein's "incorporation" does not take place anywhere; it does not entail a transfer of material from the outside to the inside; it is not part of a spatial organization; it cannot be pictured. By a strange, elemental, and in no way intellectually familiar process, a person enters into her life as a person when she learns language.

This paradox—that something "deep in us" is at the same time not part of our subjective experience but lies on the surface, "in plain view"—explains the tortuous, circling character of Wittgenstein's writing—as it battles tempting metaphors of interiorization in the context of an argument designed to exorcise the picture of a mental inside and a linguistic outside. In defiance of common sense, *Philosophical Investigations* intimates that language is not simply used by people; and Wittgenstein's efforts to circumvent metaphors of interiority sustain his subtlety in describing how people come to be by way of language, not simply by way of inventing it or being subjected to it or being formed by it but entering into it in such a way that its "depth in us" cannot be conflated with psychological interiority.

Loss of a Paradigm

Wittgenstein eschews any explicit recourse to the tragic paradigm, yet it is at work in the *Investigations* all the same. Despite his skeptical attitude toward tragic representation, it is nevertheless true that, just as Wittgenstein criticized what he was most attracted to in psychoanalysis, so he incorporated into the style, tone, and argument of *Philosophical Investigations* the sense of potential tragedy that he otherwise held up to critical examination. This sense of potential tragedy stems from Wittgenstein's evocation of groundlessness in the "forms of life" and of fragility in the language-games that provide their illusory ground. Though *Philosophical Investigations* is scrupulously antisentimental and antiexistentialist, it remains haunted by the possibility of the loss or collapse of language-games.

What does it matter that the child's primary imitation is blind? An imitation that is blind has no assured accuracy; because of the insecurity of transmission and reproduction, it will remain what I have called above an "imitation without authority" of the kind that worried Johnson: imitation whose fidelity cannot be guaranteed. In a chapter of *The Claim of Reason* entitled "Excursus on Wittgenstein's Vision of Language," Cavell tells a kind of exemplary story about the insecurity of the child's imitations: he had, to all appearances, successfully taught his infant daughter the word "kitty" when one day

> some weeks later . . . she smiled at a fur piece, stroked it, and said "kitty." My first reaction was surprise, and, I suppose, disappointment: she doesn't really know what "kitty" means. But my second reaction was happier: she means by "kitty" what I mean by "fur." Or

was it what I mean by "soft," or perhaps "nice to stroke"? Or perhaps she didn't mean at all what in my syntax would be recorded as "That is an X." (172)

Cavell tells this story to show the darkness and complexity of language acquisition, not its precariousness: his daughter's mistake was trivial, after all. But that the problem at hand is not a trivial one Cavell makes manifest in his fascination with Wittgenstein's hypothesis that the child who cannot learn our number system will be "separated out and treated like a lunatic."[2] Wittgenstein addresses the possibility of such a pedagogical breakdown when he analyses the workings of a relatively simple language-game: in response to an order from A, B is to write down a series of signs according to a certain formation rule. Here the series is that of the natural numbers:

> How does [B] get to understand this notation? First of all series of numbers will be written down for him and he will be required to copy them.... And here already there is a normal and an abnormal learner's reaction.—At first perhaps we guide his hand in writing out the series 0 to 9; but the *possibility of getting him to understand* will depend on his going on to write it down independently.—And here we can imagine, e.g., that he does copy the figures independently, but not in the right order: he writes sometimes one sometimes another at random. And then communication stops at *that* point.... Or he makes a *systematic* mistake; for example, he copies every other number, or he copies the series 0, 1, 2, 3, 4, 5 ... like this: 1, 0, 3, 2, 5, 4.... Perhaps it is possible to wean him from the systematic mistake (as from a bad habit). Or perhaps one accepts his way of copying and tries to teach him ours as an offshoot, a variant of his.— *And here too our pupil's capacity to learn may come to an end.* (no. 143; final italics mine)

What would it mean if one's capacity to learn were to "come to an end"? This failure to learn cannot be described as a failure or even a responsibility of language: what ought to secure meaning is the existence of a consistent extralinguistic self. But that cannot be found to exist. The entry into the security of language and selfhood remains highly precarious, since neither language nor memory nor even their cooperation can guarantee assurance of understanding or perpetuity of meaning. This absence of a stable self, and its consequences, provides the focus of paragraph no. 57, which describes the death of a color, its disappearance into invisibility by way of a blank in the beholder's eye:

> "Something red can be destroyed but red cannot be destroyed, and that is why the meaning of the word 'red' is independent of the existence of a red thing."—Certainly it makes no sense to say that the colour red is torn up or pounded to bits. But don't we say "The red is vanishing"? And don't clutch at the idea of our always being able to bring red before our mind's eye even when there is nothing red any more. That is just as if you chose to say that there would still always be a chemical reaction producing a red flame.—For suppose you cannot remember the colour anymore?—When we forget which colour this is the name of, it loses its meaning for us; that is, we are no longer able to play a particular language-game with it. And the situation then is comparable with that in which we have lost a paradigm which was an instrument of our language.

That we find language to move in and out of signification, and, stranger yet, that these two states cannot be sharply distinguished, Wittgenstein makes clear in many ways. I will take this discussion of "reading" as exemplifying the difficulty in question:

> Consider the following case. Human beings or creatures of some other kind are used by us as reading-machines. They are trained for this purpose. The trainer says of some that they can already read, of others that they cannot yet do so. Take the case of a pupil who has so far not taken part in the training: if he is shewn a written word he will sometimes produce some sort of sound, and here and there it happens "accidentally" to be roughly right. A third person hears this pupil on such an occasion and says: "He is reading." But the teacher says: "No, he isn't reading; that was just an accident."—But let us suppose that this pupil continues to react correctly to further words

that are put before him. After a while the teacher says: "Now he can read!"—But what of that first word? Is the teacher to say: "I was wrong, and he *did* read it"—or: "He only began really to read later on?"—When did he begin to read? Which was the first word that he *read?* This question makes no sense here.... The change when the pupil began to read was a change in his *behaviour;* and it makes no sense here to speak of "a first word in his new state." (no. 157)

The difference between an "accidentally" correct utterance and a learned skill in reading cannot be ascribed to a qualitative change in the speaker's experience: this is a corollary of the argument that "understanding" and "knowledge" are not mental states, which is to say that our use of language does not depend on an interior "experience" of meaning. This nonnecessary relationship of language to interiority explains the mysterious silence of learning language (which leads to the accident of the "kitty" story), as it also explains how we can lose "a paradigm which was an instrument of our language." Language does not represent the self; it is all the self has to show itself of meaning or understanding or interiority. Thus the charming "multiplicity of language-games" turns out to be a not wholly comforting phenomenon. As Wittgenstein elsewhere says outright, "this multiplicity is not something fixed, given once for all; but new types of language, new language-games, as we may say, come into existence, and others become obsolete and get forgotten" (no. 23).

Because of this underlying sense of melancholy, Wittgenstein's writing turns out to be oddly similar to Johnson's—a pairing that will seem less arbitrary when it is remembered that Wittgenstein described Johnson's *Prayers and Meditations* as one of his favorite books. Nor is it surprising to discover a thematic parallel in Johnson, who, from his early "Essay on the Origin and Importance of Small Tracts and Fugitive Pieces" through his *Dictionary,* edition of Shakespeare, and lives of the poets, saw it as his task to preserve from decay the ephemera of memory. The preface to the *Dictionary* naturally has the most to say about the "accidental" and "capricious" mutations to which language, memory, and the memory of language are subject: "I have ... attempted a dictionary of the English language, which, while it was employed in the cultivation of every species of literature, has itself been hitherto neglected; suffered to spread, under the direction of chance, into wild exuberance; resigned to the tyranny of time and fashion; and exposed to the corruptions of ignorance, and caprices of innovation" (*Works* 5:23). If a word such as "red" were to lose its meaning, Johnson would say that it had become an "empty sound," like the particles of a dead language, which "are suffered to pass for empty sounds, of no other use than to fill a verse or to modulate a period, but which are easily perceived in living tongues to have power and emphasis, though it be sometimes such as no other form of expression can convey" (*Works* 5:35).

Wittgenstein writes of the "mutability" to which Johnson refers, while we find in Johnson the "vanishing" of Wittgenstein's "vanishing red." Wittgenstein could imagine the color red being lost by an accident of oblivion, and moreover, he described this possibility theoretically, in his account of language as a game that no god oversees:

> Doesn't the analogy between language and games throw light here? We can easily imagine people amusing themselves in a field by playing with a ball so as to start various games, but playing many without finishing them and in between throwing the ball aimlessly into the air, chasing one another with the ball and bombarding one another for a joke and so on. And now someone says: The whole time they are playing a ball-game and following definite rules at every throw.
>
> And is there not also the case where we play and make up the rules as we go along? And there is even one where we alter them—as we go along. (no. 83)

In this strange pastoral, the transmission and reproduction of meaning are scattered to the winds. Wittgenstein describes the process lightly, invoking a lyrical rather than a tragic sense, but this model of loss and disappearance cannot help remaining ambivalent. In other moments, Wittgenstein inclined toward a more Johnsonian attitude. That there can be no guardian or witness of language's continuity, Wittgenstein emphasized with gloomy drama when he told M. O'C. Drury, "It is always a tragic thing when a language dies. But it doesn't follow that one can do anything to stop it doing so. It is a tragic thing when the love between a man and wife is dying: but there is nothing one can do. So it is with a dying language" (Rhees 138). The death of a language is the most vivid moment in a history of mnemonic insecurity. This mention of the "tragic," moreover, makes it clear that Wittgenstein's conclusions about the fragility of language-games tend to sink down of their own accord; the paradigm of the truth's grimness comes to take hold of them, and Wittgenstein's complexities of tone have to struggle, not always successfully, against the gravity of somber ideas.

In both Johnson and Shelley, as we have seen, the spirit of skepticism—that is, not metaphysical skepticism but more generally the drive to doubt and disillusionment—necessarily expresses itself in the dissolution of authority, in the work of Oedipal aggression, we might say. Wittgenstein's resistance to metaphysical skepticism does not prevent him from participating in this more amorphous form of intellectual skepticism. In Wittgenstein, too, the potential for insecurity in the definition of words—and hence its pathos—leads to the crumbling of tradition, certainty, and all their avatars. It is not merely that this tenuousness in ostensive definition reveals authority (including paternal authority, the authority of experience, and the like) to be linguistically constituted. *Philosophical Investigations* reveals the *internal* fragility of these forms of authority, which disappear at the touch. Why are they so fragile? Because they are the last, least important of language-games, as this paragraph on learning a game suggests:

> Consider this further case: I am explaining chess to someone; and I begin by pointing to a chessman and saying: "This is the king; it can move like this, . . . and so on."—In this case we shall say: the words "This is the king" (or "This is called the king") are a definition only if the learner already "knows what a piece in a game is." That is, if he has already played other games, or has watched other people playing "and understood"—*and similar things*. Further, only under these conditions will he be able to ask relevantly in the course of learning the game: "What do you call this?"—that is, this piece in a game.

We may say: only someone who already knows how to do something with it can significantly ask a name. (no. 31)

Wittgenstein chose the name of the king deliberately, in order to heighten the impotent solemnity of the ostensive definition: "This is the king." In this context, the disappointing belatedness and weakness of ostensive definition (great name of the thing, name of the great king) are brought into sharper relief by the pun—the royal father falling to the status of wood. Like the King of the Wood at Nemi, the chess king has been ceremonially overturned and undone. In fact, Wittgenstein's delicate punning of chess king and real king reminds us strangely of the claim that "the life of the priest-king shows what is meant by that phrase." Another paragraph in the *Investigations* reflects more self-consciously on this vertiginous deflation of the king. The subject is the importance of context: "A coronation is the picture of pomp and dignity. Cut one minute of this proceeding out of its surroundings: the crown is being placed on the head of the king in his coronation robes. —But in different surroundings gold is the cheapest of metals, its gleam is thought vulgar. Then the fabric of the robe is cheap to produce. A crown is a parody of a respectable hat. And so on" (no. 584). It is of course one of the major techniques of comedy to strip authority of its context and so expose it to ridicule; Wittgenstein's own humor participates in that technique. But this analysis of humor reveals at the same time its alliance with the aims of intellectual skepticism.

His choice of example reflects Wittgenstein's awareness that his project is a demystifying, or Oedipally destructive, one; the result of his investigations will be to strip away accepted truths, to deny authority, to create deprivation, disappointment, and the sense of intellectual mourning proper to the skeptical spirit. Wittgenstein already had this understanding of the effect of his thought at the time that he wrote the *Tractatus,* as one of its last, almost comical aphorisms makes clear:

The correct method in philosophy would really be the following: to say nothing except what can be said, i.e., propositions of natural science—i.e. something that has nothing to do with philosophy—and then, whenever someone else wanted to say something metaphysical, to demonstrate to him that he had failed to give a meaning to certain signs in his propositions. Although it would not be satisfying to the other person—he would not have the feeling that we were teaching him philosophy—*this* method would be the only strictly correct one. (no. 6.53)

Though Wittgenstein would later abandon the idea of any "strictly correct method," along with the rest of the *Tractatus*'s residual metaphysics, the sense of resolute asceticism remains, the sense that intellectual progress entails the surrender of habitual and comforting ideas. We recognize at once this familiar concomitant of the grimness of the truth. The *Investigations* does its own work of destruction by exposing the poverty of metaphysics, as *On Certainty* proposes to reveal the relative superficiality of metaphysical skepticism.

But at the end of his exposures, Wittgenstein has not dissolved all the power of the old forms. Though he suspected the invocation of metaphysical necessity to be spurious, his writing draws power from the hidden presence of fatefulness. *Philosophical Investigations* remains tinged with sadness because the powers of necessity and fatality have been transumed, reappearing in an unexpected place. "Acceptance" is the hidden necessity in Wittgenstein. "*What has to be accepted, the given, is—so one could say—forms of life*" (p. 226). These profoundly tenacious forms of life—"the given"—have no particular relation to truth-value, which turns out to be another latecomer on the linguistic scene. The simultaneity of living and speaking has in people the force of necessity—but other things, apparently (philosophically) more fundamental, do not: intention, truth, memory, the existence of the material world. *On Certainty* goes so far as to avow that "My *life* consists of my consenting to accept many things" (no. 344). Only the bond of accommodation between language and the forms of life ("to imagine a language means to imagine a form of life") is fated. Wittgenstein evokes a fatality that takes form so early that the proof of its existence is the randomness and fragility of everything else. *Philosophical Investigations* and *On Certainty* conjure it up without defining it and are therefore haunted by this strange form of necessity, the compulsion of this blinding origin.

> I really want to say that a language-game is only possible if one trusts something (I did not say "can trust something"). (*On Certainty* no. 509)

> "But, if you are *certain*, isn't it that you are shutting your eyes in face of doubt?"—They are shut. (*Philosophical Investigations* p. 224)

A Poetic Composition

It is true that Wittgenstein does not generally share either Johnson's lugubrious tone or Shelley's anguished one and that, in fact, he took steps to avoid striking these tones or anything like them. His lightly humorous, lyrical style is meant to divert the ponderousness of the tragic sense, though it seems often enough to slip from pastoral to pastoral elegy. Wittgenstein is more aggressively diverting with his jokes; indeed, his jokes are so wonderful that it is hard to chose favorites among them. There are hypothetical misunderstandings, such as this one: "Someone says to me: 'Shew the children a game.' I teach them gaming with dice, and the other says, 'I didn't mean that sort of game'" (*Philosophical Investigations*, p. 33). There are deflating comparisons and parables: "subjective justification"—collating your own memories—is no more trustworthy a practice than "if someone were to buy several copies of the morning paper to assure himself that what it said was true" (no. 265). There are also Wittgenstein's loonily inventive scenarios, as in the famous encounters with the man from Mars:

> I meet someone from Mars and he asks me "How many toes have human beings got?"—I say "Ten. I'll shew you," and take my shoes off. Suppose he was surprised that I knew with such certainty, although I hadn't looked at my toes—ought I to say: "We humans know how many toes we have whether we can see them or not?" (*On Certainty* no. 430)

These jokes are tendentious, of course, designed to expose the absurdity of certain commonsensical or even highly rarefied philosophical positions. They do this work, but they introduce other nuances at the same time. The charming nuttiness of the world they are adapted to describe stands out all the more vividly; it is a world of children, magically surviving in spite of their inane logic, a comic world, exposed and vulnerable. For Wittgenstein's jokes always bring back the specter of misunderstanding, delusion, error, and madness—all the possibilities of catastrophe adumbrated in the image of the pupil whose capacity to learn "has come to an end." These Kafkaesque jokes, ridiculous reimaginings of the everyday, serve to bring out some darker regularity in the forms around which their caprices dance—as befits an author of Wittgenstein's literary ambition and talent. He reputedly laughed at his own jokes in his seminars, but if anyone else laughed, he would chide them and exclaim, "This is serious!"

The literariness of Wittgenstein's writing has consequences for his argument. Pathos makes its appearance with the innocence of ordinary language, and it is increased rather than suppressed when Wittgenstein shows that "language is not a cage"—that is, that language-games are fluid and mobile, constantly changing under our blind eyes. *Philosophical Investigations* seeks to bring out the lyricism of everyday language, the beauty of what appears "in plain view." Part of this lyricism arises from the account that the *Investigations* gives of language's fragile, floating presence, and part, from the way in which the *Investigations* actually treats ordinary language as poetic. As an instance of ordinary language testimony about experience, Wittgenstein chooses the expression "In my heart I am determined on it." This example highlights the means by which *Philosophical Investigations* reveals (or re-creates) the lyricism of everyday language: through quotation, the disappearance of context. Despite Wittgenstein's well-known emphasis on the importance of context, it is the fragmentariness of these quotations that impresses them upon us and brings poignancy to his treatment of ordinary language. Removing the phrases of everyday life from their everyday contexts shows them forth in their innocent creativity, in their isolation. There is here a tenderness in the representation of language that contrasts oddly with the stern refusal of its "bewitchments." But it is this impersonal lyricism that Wittgenstein's own justly-famous prose style seeks to imitate.

Wittgenstein's suspicion of "tragic patterns" led him to aspire after a kind of pastoral in the style of *Philosophical Investigations*. The freshness of his language substantiates his ambition to escape from metaphysics into the open. And once he has abandoned metaphysics, the voice of his prose also relinquishes authority by way of namelessness. Thus his paragraphs are often made up of simple, anonymous, and strangely appealing questions. In their frankness, they make a humble yet profound claim. As a consequence, Wittgenstein's style generates an impression of warmth and intimacy but also, surprisingly, of impersonality; this is a distinctive combination worthy of Proust or Blanchot. His questions often strike an eerily direct but tentative note, as in "What does it mean to know what a game is? What does it mean, to know it and not be able to say it?" ["Was heisst es wissen, was ein Spiel ist? Was heisst es, es wissen und es nicht sagen konnen?"] (no. 75). The power of these sentences lies in their rhetorical simplicity and their seemingly unanswerable appeal. They are deliberately framed so as to sound lonely and elemental. It is because of these elemental, not necessarily answered or answerable questionings that *Philosophical Investigations* sounds naive and accessible rather than authoritative and severe.

What Wittgenstein wishes to evoke about language if not to argue about it appears in his style. Those philosophers and critics such as Richard Rorty, M. H. Abrams, and Charles Altieri who interpret the *Investigations* as a bracing exercise in common sense seem to be reading Wittgenstein's authorial voice as decided and dismissive. *Philosophical Investigations* is vulnerable to this kind of misreading. The bearing of its aphorisms can be altered dramatically by the tone of voice they are read in; but, at the same time, part of the book's stylistic novelty and power comes from the frequent absence of markers for tone. Everything is changed if Wittgenstein's open questions are read as rhetorical questions, as in this example from *On Certainty* no. 222: "I cannot possibly doubt that I was never in the stratosphere. Does that make me know it? Does it make it true?" But there is nothing to forestall such a misreading. Wittgenstein's paragraphs and quotations are orphaned; and in this way they reveal in themselves the haunting, unseen, drifting freedom of language-games.

Wittgenstein's aphorisms cultivate this elemental quality as they go about revealing the undreamt-of precedence of language-games. They are laconic, simple, and gently expressed, as if to go easy on the dreams of the metaphysics that they desolate: "Where our language suggests a body and there is none: there, we should like to say, is a *spirit*" (no. 36). This directness sometimes goes hand in hand with a gravity in the subject matter. In exploring the nominalizing picture of language and the question of whether a word has meaning only if something corresponds to it, Wittgenstein moves from the example of the sword Excalibur and its name to this rather more somber instance: "When Mr. N. N. dies one says that the bearer of the name dies, not that the meaning dies. And it would be nonsensical to say that, for if the name ceased to have meaning it would make no sense to say 'Mr. N. N. is dead'" (no. 40). The sentence "Mr. N. N. is dead" is sufficiently dramatic to float a little free of its place in the argument and to make us suddenly feel both the odd detachment and the absolute centrality of language-games. The profundity after which *Philosophical Investigations* aspires must struggle with Wittgenstein's desire to skirt the tragic sense, to maintain a playful, exploratory style that is aware of and responsive to contingency. Wittgenstein set himself the task of reconciling these two ambitions; the literary originality of his work springs from this effort, but its apparent success may be deceptive. Even in this example, the tension can be seen: there is a stimulating contrast between the gravity of the subject, which has just slipped in, and the lightness of authorial tone.

Although Wittgenstein does not discuss literary language per se, the prominence of his style makes us wonder what importance literature had for him. Its role in his thinking must be thought out in terms of his work's aspiration to the condition of literature. He put it in strong terms himself: "I think I summed up my attitude to philosophy when I said: philosophy ought really to be written only as a *poetic composition*" (*Culture and Value* 24). What does it reflect about Wittgenstein's ideas that they require themselves to be exemplified by the transformation of philosophical discourse into literary modes of persuasion? What are the consequences for those ideas that they appear in a philosophical book that treats literary style as closer to the truth of language than are the forms of explication and argumentation in conventional expository writing? Those forms are in fact represented as temptations to untruth. As Wittgenstein says in the preface to the *Investigations:* "After several unsuccessful attempts to weld my results together into . . . a whole, I realized that I should never succeed. The best that I could write would never be more than philosophical remarks; my thoughts were soon crippled if I tried to force them on in any single direction against their natural inclination." Wittgenstein settled instead for poetic "sketches of landscapes," which, he says, fearlessly turning to metaphor, "were made in the course of these long and involved journeyings." An aphorism in *Zettel* puts the case against exposition in still more poetic terms: "As one can sometimes reproduce music only in one's inward ear, and cannot whistle it, because the whistling drowns out the inner voice, so sometimes the voice of a philosophical thought is so soft that the noise of spoken words is enough to drown it and prevent it from being heard, if one is questioned and has to speak" (no. 453).³ But literary language is not merely seen as the obverse of deceptively lucid exposition: pursuing lyricism in the phrases that he studies, as well as in his own style, Wittgenstein appeals to literary affect and literary quotation to render the flavor of language's constitutive incorporation "deep in us."

As his criticism of psychoanalysis makes clear, Wittgenstein mistrusted the attraction of tragic determinism, or, we may say, of the grimness of the truth. But not when it came to literature—where this attraction has its home—for Wittgenstein appears to have been an enthusiastically naive reader, fond of dark, religious works. In the case of his favorite authors—Johnson, Tolstoy, and Dostoyevsky (like Simone Weil, he maintained a highly exclusive canon), Wittgenstein invested literature with the force of truth; he read, that is, according to the love of mimesis. We see this in the observations he is on record as having made about these authors. Johnson was able to persuade Wittgenstein of his sincerity—"I wish to say that normally I can't read any printed prayers but that Johnson's impressed me by being *human*" (Malcolm 38–39)—while, to his mind, Tolstoy portrayed the world with such accurate insight that he could be trusted as a moral authority: "Once when we were conversing Wittgenstein was delighted to learn that I knew Tolstoy's *Twenty-three Tales*. He had an extremely high opinion of these stories. He questioned me closely to find out whether I had understood the moral of the one entitled 'How Much Land Does a Man Need?'" (Malcolm 45). In Dostoyevsky Wittgenstein found still more vivid mimetic correspondences, as he reports: "When I was a village schoolmaster in Austria after the war I read *The Brothers Karamazov* over and over again. I read it out loud to the village priest. You know there really have been people like the Elder Zosima who could see into people's hearts and direct them" (Rhees 86).

Wittgenstein himself played the ethicomimetic language-game of literary interpretation and did not, therefore, treat literature as having a specially informative bearing on language. But this observation supports rather than disproves the claim that the status of literature had its effect on the argument of *Philosophical Investigations*. Under the love of mimesis, belief in literature—belief such as Wittgenstein's—tends to make itself invisible; the authority of literature is veiled by the authority of the insight with which it is being invested. The grave "truths" embodied in his favorite authors Wittgenstein saw as simply true. His intense acceptance of literature explains how and why he instinctively composed *Philosophical Investigations* in a literary form. In fact, he was conscious of this magnetism, as he reflected ruefully on the effects of his literary ambition: "I thought when I gave up my professorship that I had at last got rid of my vanity. Now I find I am vain about the style in which I am able to write my present book" (Rhees 159).

If Wittgenstein thought his favorite literature spoke truths whose truth he has only arrived at perceiving, then it is not remarkable that he chose to write *Philosophical Investigations* in a literary mode at the same time that he failed to distinguish literature theoretically. In this respect he was, so to speak, Johnson's inverse: where Johnson's suppressed but tenacious skepticism resurfaced in his mistrust of literature, Wittgenstein protected his love of literature from the skepticism over which he brooded in his philosophy. But his attraction to literature resurfaces in the ultimately tragic cast of *Philosophical Investigations*. Wittgenstein inclines toward literary style as the avatar of language's undetermined powers, only to be drawn by literature into tragic representation, because the grimness of the truth is the concept of truth—that is, the grammatical definition of the truth—that the phenomenon of literary pathos fosters.

Notes

Introduction: The Tragic Paradigm

1. All citations are from *Philosophical Investigations* unless otherwise noted. Citations from *On Certainty* and from *Philosophical Investigations* give the number for what Wittgenstein called his paragraphs or remarks. (Only part 1 of the *Investigations* is cited in this chapter.) In citations from other works of Wittgenstein, the page number is given.

2. In his excellent recent biography, Ray Monk gives an account of Wittgenstein's despair over the prestige of scientific explanation.

3. Unpublished notes of Margaret McDonald, May 22, 1935. Quoted in Cora Diamond, *The Realistic Spirit* 267.

4. Wittgenstein's critique of skepticism is discussed at greater length in chapter 6, pp. 151–52.

5. This argument depends on another: the argument that literary power is not synonymous with mimetic accuracy or the appearance of it. But that claim will not seem controversial now. In any case, one of the purposes of this book is to show how literary power can repose on affects and styles that influence or help to determine content. And these are precisely the affects and styles that go hand in hand with the assumption of the truth's harshness.

6. Compare *Philosophical Investigations* no. 217: "If I have exhausted the justifications I have reached bedrock, and my spade is turned."

Chapter 1: Weil and Aeschylus

1. This chapter is indebted to Maurice Blanchot's sympathetic treatment of Weil in *L'entretien infini*. He begins by puzzling over the charge that she lacks "rigor," when it was certainly "l'exigence rigoureuse à laquelle elle répond" (153).

2. All citations of Aeschylus refer to the OCT edition of the collected plays in Greek, *Septem Quae Supersunt Tragoedias*. The translations are my own unless otherwise identified.

3. That is, "shock" as in Johnson's protestation, "I was many years ago so shocked by Cordelia's death, that I know not whether I ever endured to read again the last scenes of the play till I undertook to revise them as an editor." The meaning of this claim is discussed in chapter 2, pp. 43–44.

4. Thomas Weiskel argues that the Kantian or negative sublime leads to so profound an alienation from sensuous reality as to issue in a suicidal ethos. See *The Romantic Sublime* 38–48.

5. See especially "Kafka et l'exigence de l'oeuvre," "Le dernier mot," and "Le tout dernier mot" in Blanchot's collection of essays titled *De Kafka à Kafka*.

Chapter 2: Johnson in Mourning

1. In *Samuel Johnson and the Tragic Sense,* Leopold Damrosch takes a rather different approach, arguing that though Johnson was sensitive to the suffering of others and "moving" in his own expressions of anguish, he sought "balance" and "breadth of vision" in art. According to Damrosch, "one is left with the persistent sense that, despite all the ways in which he was open to tragic experience, his writings constantly strive to circumvent or go beyond it" (248–49). I have not found this to be so, and the following chapters will make an argument contrary to Damrosch's. But perhaps Damrosch has assigned a narrower meaning to "tragic experience" and "tragic sense" than I have.

2. In *The Philosophical Biographer,* Martin Maner treats contradiction and ambivalence in Johnson's *Lives* rather differently, from the perspective of the contemporary interest in epistemological skepticism.

3. Compare Bronson's account of the two opposing forces in Johnson: "The conservatism of intellectual attitude and the ebullient terperament" (*Johnson Agonisties* 8).

4. Johnson seems to have found that Greek literature in particular distilled the qualities he identified with literary power. Weil and Shelley made the same association; see pp. 24 and 109.

5. Frederic Bogel's monograph *The Dream of My Brother* appeared after this essay was originally published. It covers some of the same material from Johnson's life and work (including this quotation from the "Life of Savage") in the context of the relation between authority and guilt feeling.

Chapter 3: *The Grimness of the Truth*

1. See Steven Knapp, *Personification and the Sublime.*

2. Johnson's remarks on nature and mimesis have been the subject of controversy, with some critics (such as Bate, Hagstrum, and Battersby) attempting to find a coherent literary theory behind them and others (such as Fussell) maintaining that Johnson's views are contradictory. In either case, he is imagined to have had essentially naive opinions on the relation between literature and experience (for more recent versions of this assumption, see Watt, Boyd, and Lipking). I am arguing that his love of mimesis was much deeper than theory or opinion and that it reflects a relation to literature by no means particular to Johnson.

3. The princess shortly has an opportunity to display the same regression to unfounded confidence, after being disappointed by an unideal encounter with country life: "The princess pronounced with vehemence, that she would never suffer these envious savages to be her companions, and that she should not soon be desirous of seeing any more specimens of rustick happiness" (77), yet she immediately begins to vacillate, since she cannot bring herself to "believe that all the accounts of primeval pleasures [are] fabulous"; and in spite of the evidence whose demystifying force she has just acknowledged, her fantasies of pastoral bliss spontaneously revive: "She hoped that the time would come, when with a few virtuous and elegant companions, she should gather flowers planted by her own hand, fondle the lambs of her own ewe, and listen, without care, among brooks and breezes, to one of her maidens reading in the shade" (77). No experience, however authoritative, is yet sufficient to convince the prince and princess that there is no hope. When the disheartened prince frets to find that Imlac answers his doubts "with new doubts, and remarks that [give] him no comfort," the princess encourages him to suspect Imlac's character. The teacher has his own pleasing authority to shelter, and therefore, he "favours not our search, lest we should in time find him mistaken" (89).

4. Neil Hertz drew my attention to the metrical quality of these lines.

5. There have been some excellent studies of Johnson's prose style, though none so far as I know stresses this edge of cruelty in its affect. For formalist analysis, Wimsatt's *The Prose Style of Samuel Johnson* remains standard. Isobel Grundy and William Vesterman have written incisive studies more recently. Grundy challenges Johnson's status as authority figure by analyzing the shifting, paradoxical character of his aphorisms and maxims. Aphorisms produce the appearance of "universal truth" for which Johnson's writing is famous but which, in fact, that writing is always subjecting to subtle and pervasive forms of irony.

Like Grundy, Vesterman undoes the stereotype of Johnson as an unerring, unchanging sage; he shows that Johnson's prose style became more deep, deft, and satirically powerful as it gradually abandoned the claim to transcendent authority.

    6. I owe this point to Laura Brown, who pointed out how the expectation of antithesis is defeated in these sentences.

    7. This phenomenon came up in the last chapter, where Johnson was found to produce a speech of Milton's Satan when called upon to describe his inner life.

Chapter 4: Daimonic Splendor

    1. Rajan has astutely described the complicated course of Shelley's development:

> It is evident that Shelley's poetry can be read as a suppressed debate between his idealism and his skepticism. It is tempting, moreover, to see his work as involved in a progressive deconstruction of its own assumptions. But the pattern assumed by Shelley's poetic career is not that of initial delusion followed by a progressive demystification of idealistic illusions. Rather it is a pattern of alternation between idealism and skepticism that is first confronted long before *The Triumph of Life*. The coexistence of Shelley's skepticism with his idealism reveals the compensatory and sentimental nature of this idealism and seems, therefore, to invite deconstruction. On the other hand, the alternation between skepticism and idealism is symptomatic of a certain resistance to deconstruction, which is reflected in the fact that *The Triumph of Life* is a revision rather than a reversal of *Alastor*. (*Dark Interpreter,* 83)

I find much to agree with in this strong representation. Rajan's claim that Shelley did not undergo "progressive demystification," but instead oscillated between idealism and skepticism, offers a useful antidote to more traditional but oversimplified views. Rajan is right that Shelley's poems exhibit "a pattern of alternation" rather than a process of steady and irreversible disillusionment (or enlightenment, depending on your metaphor). Yet her description of this pattern is already prejudicial, since she disparages Shelley's idealism for being "compensatory and sentimental." To represent the alternative to "deconstruction" or "demystification" as intellectually compromised is already to stack the deck, to fall in with the assumption behind the tragic paradigm that the more skeptical and discouraging conclusions are the truer. And it is perhaps to mistake the origin and intention of Shelley's "resistance to deconstruction." In a later work, *The Supplement of Reading,* Rajan modifies her argument, now maintaining that Shelley's works, rather than wavering between "naive" and "demystified" positions, exhibit a radical indeterminacy throughout.

Compare my discussion of de Man's "Shelley Disfigured," p. 142–43.

Another reading of Shelley, which bears some relation to these deconstructive readings insofar as it identifies a radical sense of indeterminacy in him, is Jerrold E. Hogle's, in *Shelley's Process*. Hogle, however, specifically disassociates his reading from deconstruction by celebrating the liberating possibilities in Shelley's discovery of "radical transference." He repudiates the implication in Rajan and de Man that Shelley's discovery falls into the category of tragic skepticism.

2. This is a somewhat unconventional interpretation; it is more usual to treat Wittgenstein's remarks on perspicuous representation as descriptive of his own modus operandi in the *Investigations*.

3. All citations of Shelley's work refer to the Reiman and Powers edition except where otherwise indicated in citation or surrounding text, and line numbers of poems (where they exist and are helpful to the reader) are given rather than page numbers. Page numbers are given for fragments, cited from *Poetical Works*. Act, scene (if there is more than one to an act), and line numbers are given for verse plays.

4. What Bloom attributes to late Shelley; see p. 142.

5. Wasserman wants to represent the argument of this poem as skeptically indeterminant, but he admits that "it is skeptical indeterminacy with a bias, for the aspiring Spirit has the best lines and the last words" (44).

6. The last word is Shelley's, from "Hymn to Intellectual Beauty": "Love, Hope and Self-esteem, like clouds depart / And come, for some uncertain moments lent" (37–38).

7. It is rare that Shelley is recognized as consciously contesting the equation of knowledge with disillusionment. In *The Romantic Sublime*, Thomas Weiskel falls into the trap of underestimating Shelley. His Shelley was too smart not to be "desublimated" but too hapless to save himself from consequent incoherence, bad faith, and despair. What Weiskel does not allow for is a perspicacious Shelley, the one who investigated and critiqued precisely the reflexive separation of creative "illusion" and desiccating knowledge. (Weiskel himself believes in this separation.) As Blake does in *The Songs of Innocence and Experience,* Shelley in his middle phase seeks to realign the divided strengths, to pair generosity with intelligence and creative power with cognitive power.

8. For a fuller discussion of style in Shelley, see William Keach, *Shelley's Style*. This fine study concentrates on figures of erosion, evanescence, speed, and instability.

9. Keach, who also discusses these revisions, puts the case succinctly: "Often in his writing about Shelley, Leavis gets hold of the right point in the wrong way"

(213). Keach agrees that the revisions increase the elegiac atmosphere of this putative love lyric.

10. See Leavis's claim that Shelley's "characteristic pathos" is "self-regarding" (220).

11. For an effective discussion of *Alastor* as a critique of Wordsworthian solipsism, see G. Kim Blank, *Wordsworth's Influence on Shelley*.

Chapter 5: Shelley's Fate

1. All citations of Shelley's work refer to the Reiman and Powers edition except where otherwise indicated in citation or surrounding text, and line numbers of poems (where they exist and are helpful to the reader) are given rather than page numbers. Page numbers are given for fragments, cited from *Poetical Works*. Act, scene (if there is more than one to an act), and line numbers are given for verse plays.

2. Shelley's late lyrics have been sensitively treated by a number of critics. Rather than major critical controversies there seem to be differences of emphasis among them. Chernaik, Bloom, and Walker concentrate on the psychological dilemmas that emerge in the poems and the innovative ways in which they are represented; Keach perceives in addition "an agitated uncertainty about writing" and "verbal representation" (233).

3. The lines have only recently come to be treated as part of the poem.

Chapter 6: Wittgenstein's Melancholy

1. All citations are from *Philosophical Investigations* unless otherwise identified. Citations from part 1 of the *Investigations* give the number for what Wittgenstein called his paragraphs, or remarks; citations from part 2 give the page number. Citations from the *Tratcatus, Zettel,* and *On Certainty* also give the paragraph number. In citations from other works of Wittgenstein, the page number is given.

2. The quotation from Wittgenstein appears in *The Blue and Brown Books* 93. Cavell discusses it in *The Claim of Reason* 112.

3. Wittgenstein puts this whole entry in parentheses, naturally.

Works Cited

Abbey, Lloyd. *Destroyer and Preserver: Shelley's Poetic Skepticism.* Lincoln: University of Nebraska Press, 1979.

Abraham, Nicholas, and Maria Torok. "A Poetics of Psychoanalysis: 'The Lost Object—Me.'" *Substance,* no. 43 (1984): 3–19.

Abrams, M. H. "How to Do Things with Texts." *Partisan Review* 46 (1979): 566–88.

Aeschylus. *Septum Quae Supersunt Tragoedias.* Ed. Denys Page. Oxford: Oxford University Press, 1972.

Altieri, Charles. "Wittgenstein on Consciousness and Language: A Challenge to Derridean Literary Theory." *Modern Language Notes* 91 (1974): 1397–1424.

Aristophanes. *Ranae.* Ed. F. A. Paley. Cambridge: Deighton, Bell, 1877.

———. "The Frogs." In *Four Plays by Aristophanes,* trans. William Arrowsmith et al. New York: NAL, 1962.

Austin, J. L. *How To Do Things with Words.* 2nd edition. Cambridge, Mass.: Harvard University Press, 1975.

Bate, W. Jackson. *The Achievement of Samuel Johnson.* Chicago: University of Chicago Press, 1978.

———. *Samuel Johnson.* New York: Harcourt Brace Jovanovich, 1977.

Battersby, James L. *Rational Praise and Natural Lamentation: Johnson, "Lycidas," and Principles of Criticism.* Rutherford, N.J.: Fairleigh Dickinson University Press; London: Associated University Presses, 1980.

Benjamin, Walter. *Illuminations.* Ed. Hannah Arendt. Trans. Harry Zohn. New York: Schocken, 1969.

Bishop, Elizabeth. *The Complete Poems, 1927–1979.* New York: Farrar, Straus, and Giroux, 1979.

Blanchot, Maurice. *L'entretien infini.* Paris: Gallimard, 1969.

———. *De Kafka à Kafka.* Paris: Gallimard, 1981.

Blank, G. Kim. *Wordsworth's Influence on Shelley: A Study of Poetic Authority.* New York: St. Martin's Press, 1988.

Bloom, Harold. Introduction to *Percy Bysshe Shelley: Modern Critical Views.* Ed. Harold Bloom, 1–29. New York: Chelsea House, 1985.

———. *The Visionary Company.* Ithaca: Cornell University Press, 1970.

Bogel, Fredric V. *The Dream of My Brother: An Essay on Johnson's Authority.* ELS Monograph Series, no. 47. Victoria, B.C.: University of Victoria Press, 1990.
Boyd, John D., S.J. "Some Limits in Johnson's Literary Criticism." In *Johnson and His Age,* ed. James Engell, 191–215. Harvard English Studies, no. 12. Cambridge, Mass.: Harvard University Press, 1984.
Boswell, James. *The Life of Samuel Johnson, LL.D.* 2nd edition. Ed. R. W. Chapman; rev. J. D. Fleeman. Oxford: Oxford University Press, 1953.
Bronson, Bertrand. *Johnson Agonistes and Other Essays.* Cambridge: Cambridge University Press, 1946.
Burke, Edmund. *A Philosophical Enquiry into the Origin of Our Ideas of the Sublime and Beautiful.* Ed. Adam Phillips. Oxford: Oxford University Press, 1990.
Cavell, Stanley. *The Claim of Reason: Wittgenstein, Skepticism, Morality, and Tragedy.* Oxford: Clarendon; New York: Oxford University Press, 1979.
Chernaik, Judith. *The Lyrics of Shelley.* Cleveland: Case Western Reserve University Press, 1972.
Damrosch, Leopold. *Samuel Johnson and the Tragic Sense.* Princeton: Princeton University Press, 1972.
Davie, Donald. "Shelley's Urbanity." In *Purity of Diction in English Verse,* 133–60. London: Routledge and Kegan Paul, 1967.
Deleuze, Gilles. "Nomad Thought." *Semiotexte* 3, no. 1 (1978): 12–20.
de Man, Paul. "Hegel on the Sublime." In *Displacement: Derrida and After,* ed. Mark Krupnick, 139–53. Bloomington: Indiana University Press, 1983.
——— . "Shelley Disfigured." In *The Rhetoric of Romanticism,* 93–123. New York: Columbia University Press, 1984.
Diamond, Cora. *The Realistic Spirit: Wittgenstein, Philosophy, and the Mind.* Cambridge, Mass.: MIT Press, 1991.
Ferguson, Frances. *Solitude and the Sublime: Romanticism and the Aesthetics of Individuation.* New York: Routledge, 1992.
Fitzgerald, F. Scott. *The Crack-Up.* New York: New Directions, 1931.
Fussell, Paul. *Samuel Johnson and the Life of Writing.* New York: Norton, 1971.
Grundy, Isobel. "Samuel Johnson: Man of Maxims." In *Samuel Johnson: New Critical Essays,* ed. Isobel Grundy, 13–30. London: Vision, 1984.
Hagstrum, Jean H. *Samuel Johnson's Literary Criticism.* Chicago: University of Chicago Press, 1967.
Hazlitt, William. "On the Periodical Essayists." In *Lectures on the English Comic Writers,* 91–105. London: Dent, 1910.
Herrington, John. *Aeschylus.* New Haven: Yale University Press, 1986.

Hertz, Neil. *The End of the Line: Essays on Psychoanalysis and the Sublime.* New York: Columbia University Press, 1985.

Hirschman, Albert O. *The Rhetoric of Reaction: Perversity, Futility, Jeopardy.* Cambridge, Mass.: Belknap Press of Harvard University Press, 1991.

Hogle, Jerrold E. *Shelley's Process: Radical Transference and the Development of His Major Works.* Oxford: Oxford University Press, 1988.

Holmes, Richard. *Shelley: The Pursuit.* London: Weidenfeld and Nicolson, 1974.

Johnson, Samuel. *Diaries, Prayers, and Annals.* Ed. E. L. McAdam, Jr., with Donald and Mary Hyde. Vol. 1 of the *Yale Edition of the Works of Samuel Johnson.* 14 vols. to date. New Haven: Yale University Press, 1978.

———. *The Idler and The Adventurer.* Ed. W. J. Bate, John M. Bullitt, and L. F Powell. Vol. 2 of the *Yale Edition of the Works of Samuel Johnson.* New Haven: Yale University Press, 1963.

———. *Johnson on Shakespeare.* Ed. Arthur Sherbo. Vols. 7 and 8 of the *Yale Edition of the Works of Samuel Johnson.* New Haven: Yale University Press, 1968.

———. *The Letters of Samuel Johnson.* Ed. Bruce Redford. 5 vols. Princeton: Princeton University Press, 1982–94.

———. *Lives of the English Poets.* 2 vols. Oxford.: Oxford University Press, 1906.

———. *Poems.* Ed. E. L. McAdam, Jr., with George Milne. Vol. 6 of the *Yale Edition of the Works of Samuel Johnson.* New Haven: Yale University Press, 1964.

———. *The Rambler.* Ed. W. J. Bate and Albrecht B. Strauss. Vols. 3, 4, and 5 of the *Yale Edition of the Works of Samuel Johnson.* New Haven: Yale University Press, 1969.

———. *Rasselas and Other Tales.* Ed. Gwin J. Kolb. Vol. 16 of the *Yale Edition of the Works of Samuel Johnson.* New Haven: Yale University Press, 1990.

———. *Sermons.* Ed. Jean Hagstrum and James Gray. Vol. 14 of the *Yale Edition of the Works of Samuel Johnson.* New Haven: Yale University Press, 1978.

———. *The Works of Samuel Johnson, L.L.D.* 9 vols. Oxford: Talboys and Wheeler, 1825.

Keach, William. *Shelley's Style.* New York: Methuen, 1984.

Klein, Melanie. *Love, Guilt and Reparation & Other Works 1921–1945.* New York: Delta-Dell, 1975.

Knapp, Steven. *Personification and the Sublime: Milton to Coleridge.* Cambridge, Mass.: Harvard University Press, 1985.

Lacoue-Labarthe, Philippe. "Sublime Truth (Part 1)." *Cultural Critique* 18 (Spring 1991): 5–31.

———. "Sublime Truth (Part 2)." *Cultural Critique* 20 (Winter 1991–92): 207–29.
Leavis, F. R. *Revaluation*. London: Chatto and Windus, 1969.
Lipking, Lawrence. "Johnson and the Meaning of Life." In *Johnson and His Age*, ed. James Engell, 1–27. Harvard English Studies, no. 12. Cambridge, Mass.: Harvard University Press, 1984.
Malcolm, Norman. *Ludwig Wittgenstein: A Memoir*. 2nd edition. Oxford: Oxford University Press, 1984.
Maner, Martin. *The Philosophical Biographer: Doubt and Dialectic in Johnson's "Lives of the Poets."* Athens: University of Georgia Press, 1988.
Milton, John. *Complete Poems and Major Prose*. Ed. Merritt Y. Hughes. Bloomington: Indiana University Press, 1957.
Monk, Ray. *Ludwig Wittgenstein: The Duty of Genius*. New York: Press, 1990.
O'Neill, Michael. *The Human Mind's Imaginings: Conflict and Achievement in Shelley's Poetry*. Oxford: Oxford University Press, 1989.
Piozzi, Hester Lynch [Mrs. Thrale]. *Anecdotes of Samuel Johnson*. Ed. S. C. Roberts. Cambridge: Cambridge University Press, 1932.
Pulos, C. E. *The Deep Truth: A Study of Shelley's Scepticism*. Lincoln: University of Nebraska Press, 1962.
Rajan, Tilottama. *Dark Interpreter: The Discourse of Romanticism*. Ithaca: Cornell University Press, 1980.
———. *The Supplement of Reading: Figures of Understanding in Romantic Theory and Practice*. Ithaca: Cornell University Press, 1990.
Rhees, Rush, ed. *Recollections of Wittgenstein*. Oxford: Oxford University Press, 1984.
Rorty, Richard. *Consequences of Pragmatism: Essays, 1972–80*. Minneapolis: University of Minnesota Press, 1982.
Sachs, Arieh. *Passionate Intelligence: Imagination and Reason in the Work of Samuel Johnson*. Baltimore: Johns Hopkins University Press, 1967.
Searle, John R. "Reiterating the Differences: A Reply to Derrida." *Glyph* 1 (1977): 198–208.
Shelley, Percy. *Letters*. Ed. F. L. Jones. 2 vols. London: Oxford University Press, 1964.
———. *Poetical Works*. Ed. Thomas Hutchinson. London: Oxford University Press, 1970.
———. *Shelley's Poetry and Prose*. Ed. Donald H. Reiman and Sharon B. Powers. New York: Norton, 1977.
———. *Shelley's Prose, or The Trumpet of a Prophecy*. Ed. David Lee Clark. Albuquerque: University of New Mexico Press, 1954.

Vesterman, William. *The Stylistic Life of Samuel Johnson.* New Brunswick, N.J.: Rutgers University Press, 1977.

Virgil. *The Aeneid.* Trans. Allen Mandelbaum. Berkeley: University of California Press, 1981.

Walker, Constance. "Shelley's Portrayals of Emotion in the Lyrics to Jane Williams." In *Approaches to Teaching Shelley's Poetry.* Ed. Spencer Hall. New York: Modern Language Association, 1990.

Wasserman, Earl. R. *Shelley: A Critical Reading.* Baltimore: Johns Hopkins University Press, 1971.

Watkins, W. B. C. *Perilous Balance: The Tragic Genius of Swift, Johnson, and Sterne.* Princeton: Princeton University Press, 1939.

Watt, Ian. "Dr. Johnson and the Literature of Experience." In *Johnsonian Studies,* ed. Magdi Wahba, 15–22. Cairo: Société orientale de publicité, 1962.

Weil, Simone. *Attente de Dieu.* Paris: Fayard, 1966.

———. *Gravity and Grace.* Trans. Arthur Wills. New York: Putnam, 1952.

———. *Seventy Letters.* Ed. and trans. Richard Rees. New York: Oxford University Press, 1965.

———. *The Simone Weil Reader.* Ed. George A. Panichas. New York: McKay, 1977.

———. *La Source Grecque.* Paris: Gallimard, 1953.

Weiskel, Thomas. *The Romantic Sublime: Studies in the Structure and Psychology of Transcendence.* New Haven: Yale University Press, 1976.

Wharton, T. F. *Samuel Johnson and the Theme of Hope.* London: Macmillan, 1984.

Wimsatt, W. K., Jr. *The Prose Style of Samuel Johnson.* New Haven: Yale University Press, 1941.

Wittgenstein, Ludwig. *The Blue and Brown Books.* Oxford: Blackwell, 1958.

———. *Culture and Value.* Ed. G. H. von Wright. Trans. Peter Winch. Chicago: University of Chicago Press, 1980.

———. *Lectures and Conversations on Aesthetics, Psychology and Religious Belief.* Ed. Cyril Barrett. Berkeley and Los Angeles: University of California Press, n.d.

———. "Lecture on Ethics." *Philosophical Review* 74 (1965): 3–26.

———. *On Certainty.* Ed. G. E. M. Anscombe and G. H. von Wright. Trans. Denis Paul and G. E. M. Anscombe. New York: Harper, 1972.

———. *Philosophical Investigations.* Trans. G. E. M. Anscombe. 3rd ed. New York: Macmillan, 1968.

———. *Remarks on Frazer's "Golden Bough."* Ed. Rush Rhees. Trans. A. C. Miles. Retford, Eng.: Brynmill; Atlantic Highlands, N.J.: Humanities Press, 1983.

———. *Tractatus Logico-Philosophicus.* Trans. D. F. Pears and B. F. McGuiness. London: Routledge and Kegan Paul, 1961.

———. *Zettel.* Ed. G. E. M. Anscombe and G. H. von Wright. Trans. G. E. M. Anscombe. Berkeley and Los Angeles: University of California Press, 1967.

Zizek, Slavoj. *The Sublime Object of Ideology.* London: Verso, 1989.

Index

Abbey, Lloyd, 88
Abraham, Nicholas, 52
Abrams, M. H., 164
Aeschylus, 12, 16–24, 109, 142
Altieri, Charles, 164
Aristophanes, 18–21, 24
Augustine, Saint, 150, 152–53

Bate, Walter Jackson, 30
Beckett, Samuel, xix
Benjamin, Walter, 84
Bishop, Elizabeth, 134–35
Blake, William, 137
Blanchot, Maurice, xvii, 26, 66, 164, 169n.
Blank, G. Kim, 174n.
Bloom, Harold, xvi, 88, 105, 142, 173n., 174n.
Bogel, Frederic, 170n.
Boswell, John, 37, 40, 48, 52–53, 56, 66–67, 80
Boyd, John D., 171n.
Bronson, Bertrand, 170n.
Brontë, Charlotte, 55
Brown, Laura, 172n.
Burke, Edmund, xiii–xiv, xvii, 25
Byron. *See* Gordon, George

Cavell, Stanley, 152, 154–55, 174n.
Chekhov, Anton, xix
Clairemont, Claire, 143
Cowley, Abraham, 30–33, 45, 60–64

Damrosch, Leopold, 170n.
Deleuze, Gilles, xv
de Man, Paul, xvi–xvii, 20, 88, 142
Descartes, René, 148
Diamond, Cora, 169n.
Dostoyevsky, Fyodor, 166–67

Dryden, John, 82

Ecclesiastes, 118–19
Euripides, 19–21, 39–40

Fate, 4, 17, 18, 21–24, 26, 40, 72
Ferguson, Frances, xvi
Fielding, Henry, 49
Fitzgerald, F. Scott, 26
Frazer, James, 1–2
Freud, Sigmund, 3–5, 6, 145, 150

Gay, John, 48
Generalization, 4, 6–9, 29, 90, 91–92, 95–98, 119, 121–22, 138, 141–42
Gordon, George, Lord Byron, 138
Grimness of the truth, The, xiv, xix, 8–10, 17, 20–21, 56, 59–60, 87, 90–91, 99, 107, 113, 123–24, 142, 144, 166–67
Grundy, Isobel, 171–72n.

Hagstrum, Jean H., 171n.
Hardy, Thomas, xix
Herrington, John, 23
Hertz, Neil, xvi, 171n.
Hirschman, Albert O., 104
Hogle, Jerrold E., 173n.
Homer, xix, 16, 56–57
Hume, David, xv

Johnson, Samuel, xviii–xix, 8–10, 13, 15, 29–85, 87, 89–92, 96–98, 109, 115, 119, 157–58, 162, 166–67, 170n.
—Works: Diaries, 38–39, 76; *Dictionary*, 37, 50–51, 157–58; "Essay on the Origin and Importance of

Small Tracts and Fugitive Pieces," 157; *Idler, The* 58, 71; *Johnson on Shakespeare*, 40–41, 43–48, 50, 65, 157; Letters, 42–43, 48, 51, 58, 76, 78; *Lives of the Poets*, 30–39, 44–45, 52–53, 58–66, 71–72, 77, 84, 157; *Prayers and Meditations*, 46, 157; *Rambler, The* 31, 35, 41–42, 46, 49–51, 56–57, 60, 65–68, 71–73, 78–80; *Rasselas*, 30, 49–51, 55, 67, 72, 74–76, 78, 119; Sermons, 37–38; "Vanity of Human Wishes, The," 22, 72, 74–77, 95, 119

Kafka, Franz, xvii, 26
Kant, Immanuel, xv
Keach, William, 174n.
Knapp, Steven, 171n.

Lacoue-Labarthe, Philippe, xvi
Leavis, F. R., 116–17, 121, 174n.
Lipking, Lawrence, 171n.
Longinus, xvi

Maner, Martin, 170n.
Martial, 81–82
Milton, John, xiv, 32–37, 45–46, 52, 64–66, 82, 92, 101, 126, 172n.
Mimesis, 9–10, 19–20, 25–26, 56–67, 83–84
Monk, Ray, 169n.
Mourning, 29–36, 52, 64, 84, 160

O'Neill, Michael, 108
Otway, Thomas, 58–60

Pathos, xv, 8, 11, 33, 36, 39–40, 42–44, 51, 56, 59, 67, 83, 163, 167
Perspicuous representation. *See* "Wide survey"
Phillips, Ambrose, 77
Piozzi, Hester Thrale, 39, 73, 77
Plato, 16–17

Pope, Alexander, 59, 63, 84
Proust, Marcel, xvii, 66, 104
Pulos. C. E., 88–89

Rajan, Tilortama, 88, 172n.
Richardson, Samuel, xv
Rorty, Richard, 164
Rousseau, Jean-Jacques, 142

Sachs, Arieh, 29
St. John of the Cross, xix, 17
Savage, Richard, 44–45
Severity, 3, 8, 11–12, 18, 21, 24, 26–27, 29, 55–56, 67–80, 85, 90, 92, 95–97, 123–24, 129, 141
Shakespeare, William, xix, 45, 47, 50, 67, 82–83, 101
—Works: *Hamlet*, 80–81; *King Lear*, xv, 7, 14–6, 40–41, 44, 55, 170n.; *Othello*, 40; *Tempest, The* xv
Shelley, Mary, 143–44
Shelley, Percy Bysshe, xviii–xix, 8–0, 26, 87–44, 159, 162, 170n.
—Works: "An Address to the People on the Death of Princess Charlotte," 113; *Adonais*, 89, 95, 98, 101, 114, 121, 123–25, 127, 141, 144; "Alas! this is not what I thought life was," 141; *Alastor*, 98, 119–20, 140; *Cenci, The* 98; *Defense of Poetry, The* 98, 100–1; *Epipsychidion*, 114, 117, 128, 142; "Flower That Smiles Today, The" 101; *Hellas*, 92–93, 114; "Hymn to Intellectual Beauty," 110–11; "Invitation, The," 116, 128; *Julian and Maddalo*, 98, 105, 107–8, 140; Letters, 90, 143; "Lift Not the Painted Veil," 118–21, 140; "Lines Written in the Bay of Lerici," 113, 123, 127–40; "Magnetic Lady to Her Patient, The" 128, 131; *Mask of Anarchy, The*, 112–13; "Mont Blanc," 110, 115; "Mutability," 96, 123–24; "Ode to Heaven,"

93–95; "Ode to the West Wind," 110–12; "On Death," 119, 123; "Ozymandias," 127; *Peter Bell the Third*, 120; "Pine Forest of the Cascine Near Pisa, The," 116; *Prometheus Unbound*, xv, 87, 94–95, 98, 101–9, 113–15, 124; *Queen Mab*, 92; "Recollection, The," 116–17, 128, 139; "Song of Apollo," 126; "Song of Pan," 126–27; "Stanzas Written in Dejection," 107; "To a Skylark," 110; "To Jane," 114, 128, 139; "To Night," 114–15; "Serpent Is Shut Out from Paradise, The," 139; *Triumph of Life, The*, xv, 89, 98, 105, 114, 119, 123–26, 128, 140, 142–43; "Two Spirits: An Allegory, The," 98–101, 105; "When Passion's Trance is Overpast," 97, 101; "With a Guitar. To Jane," 128, 139, 143; "Written on Hearing the News of the Death of Napoleon," 113–14; "Ye Hasten to the Grave," 123; "Zucca, The," 111, 140
Skepticism, xix, 8–9, 29, 88–95, 98, 107, 111, 115, 121–22, 140, 144, 151–52, 159–62, 167, 170n.
Smollett, Tobias, 49
Solitude, 30, 33, 40–41, 47, 51–52, 81
Sophocles, 17, 23
Sublime, The, xiii–xvi, 5–6, 8, 25, 98, 101, 107, 123–24, 144
Swift, Jonathan, 81

Tate, Nahum, 40–41
Torok, Maria, 52
Tragic paradigm, xvi–xvii, 1–3, 7–2, 87, 90–91, 98–109, 145, 154

Tragic sense, xiii, xv–xvii, 11, 29, 87, 105, 145, 162

Uncanny, The, 3, 24, 30, 113, 144

Vesterman, William, 171–72n.
Virgil, 56–57, 81

Walker, Constance, 174n.
Wasserman, Earl, 88–89, 108, 173n.
Watkins, W. B. C., 30
Watt, Ian, 171n.
Weil, Simone, xviii–xix, 10, 13–27, 29–30, 59, 84, 109, 115, 143, 166, 169n., 170n.
—Works: *Attente de Dieu*, 13, 16, 25; *Gravity and Grace*, 14, 27; *Seventy Letters*, 13–5; *La Source Grecque*, 14, 17
Weiskel, Thomas, xvi, 170n., 173n.
Wharton, T. F., 30
"Wide survey," 22, 62, 72, 77, 90–95, 118, 126
Wimsatt, W. K., 171n.
Wittgenstein, Ludwig, xvii–xix, 1–2, 22, 91–92, 98, 101, 115, 145–67
—Works: *Culture and Value*, 165; jokes, 162–63; *Lectures and Conversations on Aesthetics*, 3, 145; *On Certainty*, 8, 150–52, 161–62, 164; *Philosophical Investigations*, xvi, 2–3, 5–7, 10, 12, 92, 145–50, 152–67; *Remarks on Frazer's Golden Bough*, 1–2; *Tractatus Logico-Philosophicus*, 5–6, 145, 147, 160–61; *Zettel*, 166
Wordsworth, William, 119–20, 142
Wyatt, Thomas, xix

Zizek, Slavoj, xvi